By

EVAN H. FARR
CERTIFIED ELDER LAW ATTORNEY

*Obtaining **True** Asset Protection by Protecting Your Assets from Probate **PLUS** Lawsuits **PLUS** Nursing Home Expenses*

Library of Congress Control Number: 2013904871

ISBN: 978-0-9761821-3-9

First Printing June 2013

Published by
Quality Legal Publications, LLC
Fairfax, Virginia

Quality Legal
Publications

Dedicated to My Biggest Fans:

My Wife, Jeannie

My Son, Timothy

My Life Guide, Jonathan

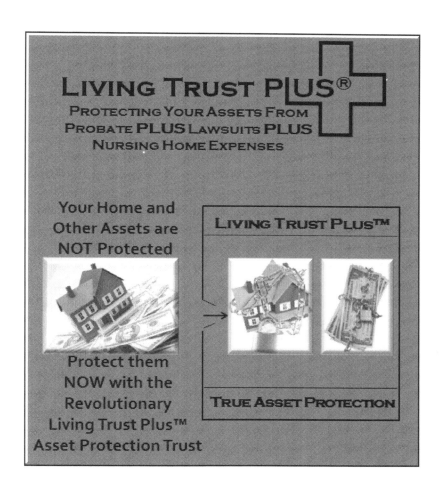

Table of Contents

FORWARD

Most people doing estate planning use a revocable living trust to avoid the hassles and expenses of probate. There are hundreds of books and thousands of Web sites devoted to the revocable living trust, and it is widely recognized by attorneys and consumers that a revocable living trust is tremendously superior to a last will and testament as an estate planning tool. This book will not attempt to explore in depth all of the benefits of a revocable living trust, but will highlight some. Readers not familiar with all of the benefits of a revocable living trust should obtain one of the many other excellent books on this topic.

One of the best is the seminal book on the topic – **The Living Trust: The Failproof Way to Pass Along Your Estate to Your Heirs,** by Henry Abst. Mr. Abst essentially created the revocable living trust industry when he published his book back in 1989, which quickly became and still is the "bible" on how to avoid probate. I remember it, because I started practice back in 1987, two years before his book came out, and at that time no one was doing living trusts; they were essentially unheard of. Even though Living Trusts had been used as far back as 16th century England, Mr. Abst came along just 20 years ago, put together all the puzzle pieces, wrote a book explaining it, and completely revolutionized the estate planning industry.

Although a revocable living trust does a terrific job of avoiding probate, what most people don't realize is that a revocable living trust does not protect your assets from creditors or from the expenses of long-term care.

With this book, my goal is to do the same thing for the Living Trust Plus™ that Mr. Abst did for the revocable living trust. I hope to revolutionize the Estate Planning industry by making the Living Trust Plus™ a universally-recognized estate planning alternative – the alternative that provides consumers with all the best features of a regular living trust PLUS the extra and vital benefit of asset protection that consumers are so hungry for, especially in this recovering economy where most Americans have recently seen their life savings gutted.

This book will explain how to use the Living Trust Plus™ to avoid the problems of probate PLUS lawsuits PLUS long term care. In doing so, I will first explain the problems of probate and the risks of lawsuits and long term care. Then I'll start looking at the possible solutions. First, we'll look at whether Wills offer a solution. Second, we'll look at joint ownership and beneficiary designations. Lastly, I'll talk about living trusts – both the regular living trust (i.e., the revocable living trust that Mr. Abst wrote about and that almost everybody has heard of, designed primarily to avoid probate) and more importantly, the Living Trust Plus™.

I created Living Trust Plus™ in 2006 for my clients, and it is now being used by dozens of exceptional estate planning and elder law attorneys throughout the country. The Living Trust Plus™ is a trust that is specifically designed to avoid the expenses and devastation of probate PLUS lawsuits PLUS long term care.

Evan H. Farr, CELA

Certified as an Elder Law Attorney by the National Elder Law Foundation
Creator of the Living Trust Plus™: http://www.LivingTrustPlus.com
Farr Law Firm, 10640 Main Street, Suite 200, Fairfax, VA 22030
VirginiaElderLaw.com   &   VirginiaEstatePlanning.com
Daily Blog: blog.EverythingElderLaw.com
Weekly Blog: blog.ElderLawPlus.com
703-691-1888 or 1-800-399-FARR

Virginia has no procedure for approving certifying organizations.

chapter 1

THE PROBLEM OF PROBATE

Almost everyone has heard of "the nightmare of probate." The two words just go together. You hardly ever hear about probate without hearing about the "nightmare of probate" because probate really is, for the most part, almost always a nightmare.

Basically, probate is a complex, expensive, court-supervised process that many families are forced to go through when a loved one becomes incapacitated during lifetime, or when a loved one dies. Probate occurs whether your loved one becomes incapacitated and does not have a General Power of Attorney, or dies without a Will ("intestate"), or dies with a Will (testate). Consider the following case study.

PROBATE CASE STUDY

• Background

Mary Johnson is an 84-year old widow with three children – Joan, Sam, and Bill. Joan and Sam are both trustworthy and responsible adults and have maintained a loving relationship with Mary over the years. Joan is a nurse in a doctor's office and Sam works as an advertising executive. Bill, unfortunately, has had a checkered past – he's never held a job for more than a year, has had serious financial problems, has spent time in jail for theft

> *Probate is a complex, expensive, court-supervised process that many families are forced to go through when a loved one dies or becomes incapacitated.*

(including stealing a significant sum of money from Mary), and has had no contact with the rest of the family for the past 15 years.

Mary's husband, John, died 3 years ago. John died intestate, meaning he had never written a Will, and when he died, his estate had to go into probate because John had several accounts that did not have Mary's name on them. Mary had paid a lawyer over ten thousand dollars to have John's estate probated so all of John's accounts could be put into her name, and Mary didn't want her children to have to go through all that hassle and expense when she died.

So Mary asked the lawyer to draw up a Will for her, assuming that the Will would avoid the expenses and hassles of probate that she had gone through with John's estate. She told the attorney to name her children Joan and Sam as the beneficiaries of her Will and to name Joan to be the Executor of her Will. Since Mary didn't want to leave anything to Bill, she didn't bother mentioning Bill to the attorney. At the attorney's suggestion, Mary also signed Incapacity Planning documents – a General Power of Attorney and an Advance Medical Directive. The lawyer explained that these documents were important for avoiding lifetime probate if Mary were to become incapacitated. Unfortunately the lawyer did not explain that Mary's Will would simply put her estate through probate after her death, because he just assumed Mary understood that.

Mary was very pleased to tell Joan and Sam that she'd set up everything with the lawyer to make things as easy as possible for Joan and Sam after her death, not realizing that the Will she signed was NOT going to avoid probate, but rather was going to put her estate through probate.

One year after her husband's death, Mary fell and broke her hip, an extremely common occurrence among women Mary's age. After undergoing hip surgery, Mary spent 4 days in the hospital and was then transferred to a nearby nursing facility for rehabilitation. At first, Mary did the best she could to participate in all of the exercises the physical therapists wanted her to do. But then, about two weeks after the surgery, Mary developed pneumonia, a very serious complication after major surgery, and she was so weakened after contracting pneumonia that she felt unable to participate in the physical therapy.

Tragically, Mary's condition continued to worsen and her weakened condition led to her not being able to leave the nursing home. As happens to so many elders, Mary wound up staying at the nursing home and simply transitioning from short-term rehabilitation in to long-term care. Although she recovered from the pneumonia, Mary never regained her strength, and her condition slowly deteriorated over the ensuing months and years. After almost 3 years in the nursing home, Mary fell again and broke the same hip she had broken earlier. After being hospitalized and undergoing another surgery, Mary again developed pneumonia and also suffered some additional complications from the surgery. This time, Mary was too weak to recover from the surgery and all of the complications. She died just one week after the surgery.

- **The First Step in Probate - A Trip to the Courthouse**

After Mary's death, Joan makes an appointment to see the attorney who handled her father's estate and drew up her mother's Will. Joan is horrified to find out that Mary's Will must be admitted to probate.

Mary's assumption that a Will would avoid probate (an assumption shared by Joan) was completely wrong. The attorney explains that the whole purpose of a Will is to give instructions to the probate court. A Will, the attorney explained correctly, doesn't even become effective until it's accepted by the probate court as valid and admitted to probate, thereby commencing the probate process.

> *A Will doesn't become effective until it's accepted by the probate court as valid and admitted to probate, thereby commencing the probate process.*

The probate process differs from state to state, and the process is more complicated in some states than others. This story is an example of the probate process in Virginia.

Disgusted with the attorney for never explaining all of this to her mother, Joan decides to handle the probate process herself. So she takes her mother's Will and death certificate to the courthouse and sits down to talk to the probate clerk for an hour or two, filling out lots of forms and answering lots of questions. The end result of this initial courthouse visit is that Joan gets a certificate stating that she has been officially appointed by the court as the Executor of Mary's Will, along with a three-inch thick manila envelope full of forms and instructions, statutes and samples, explaining all her duties as the Executor of Mary's estate.

To fulfill her duties, Joan will have to complete and file a lot of legal forms with the probate court. Some are relatively easy; others, as Joan will soon find out, are incredibly complicated.

• The Real Estate Wait

One of the first things Joan wants to do is clean out Mary's house and get it ready for sale. Joan contacts a cleaning company, a moving company, and an auction company to deal with all of Mary's household belongings. Then she hires a real estate agent and lists the house for sale. At the closing on the sale of the house, Joan is dismayed to learn that the net proceeds from the sale of the house will have to be held in escrow by the title company for a year before the proceeds can actually be paid to the estate. This is because of a state law that says the proceeds from the sale of real estate are subject to debts of the estate for a one-year period.

• The Probate Filing Fiasco

Joan's visit to the probate court was just the beginning of a lengthy, complex, tedious, and expensive process. Now that she's gone to court and been appointed as the Executor of her mother's Will, she needs to start filling out and filing all of the required legal documents.

• Notices to Ne'er-do-wells

The first thing Joan needs to file is the Notice to Heirs. Joan is again horrified – this time to find out from the Court Clerk that the term "heirs" includes her brother Bill. Even though Mary did not leave anything to Bill, Mary's heirs are all of her children (Bill included) because her heirs are the people who would inherit her estate if she had died without a Will. The Court Clerk explains to Joan that the state has written a simple will for everyone that says if your spouse has predeceased you then "everything goes to your children in equal shares." So even though Mary intended to

Even though Mary intended to disinherit Bill, he is still one of her heirs, and because her estate has wound up in probate, Bill must be notified that Mary died. Worse yet, once Bill receives that notice, he'll be given ample opportunity to contest her Will.

disinherit Bill, he is still one of her heirs, and because her estate has wound up in probate, Bill must be notified that Mary died. Worse yet, once Bill receives that notice, he'll be given ample opportunity to contest her Will.

• The Illusive Inventory

After sending the notices to all of the heirs and filing an affidavit with the probate court certifying that she sent the notices, Joan must file a second legal document with the probate court, called an Inventory of the estate. The Inventory is due four months after Joan first went to court to become the Executor of her mother's estate. The Inventory Joan must file is an itemized listing of all the assets that Mary owned as of the date of her death and the exact value of all those assets as of that date. For Mary's real estate, that means getting an appraisal. Mary's financial assets were a checking account and a savings account with her local bank, a brokerage account, a money market account, a Certificate of Deposit, and 100 shares of stock in the Arlington Community Bank that Mary's husband had purchased over 30 years earlier. Adding all of her financial assets to the value of Mary's real estate, Mary died with an estate worth approximately $300,000. Her estate would have been almost double that except that Mary's 3 years in the nursing home had cost almost $100,000 per year.

For each financial asset, Joan writes the financial institution to ask for the exact value of every asset as of the date of death. After six months, the financial institution holding the money market account still hasn't responded, and Joan remains unable to determine what to do about the bank stock because the bank in question hasn't existed for at least 25 years, having been the subject of numerous mergers and acquisitions over the years.

About 18 months and dozens of hours of research later, Joan finally determines which "megabank" is the successor to the old bank stock, but when Joan contacts the megabank they tell her they'll have to do their own research to figure out how much the stock is worth. Another 18 months will go by and Joan will still have heard nothing from the bank about the stock.

After another number of months, Joan will have also written 5 letters and made half a dozen phone calls to the institution holding the money market and will still never have gotten the date of death value of the money market, meaning that even after 3 years from Mary's death, Joan still won't be able to finalize the inventory or close the probate estate.

- **The Abhorrent Accounting**

But wait – it gets worse! Joan must start filing accountings with the probate court sixteen months after the probate process began, and then annually every year after that. This despite the fact that Joan has not been able to finalize the inventory of the estate. It is the annual accounting that is the most complex part of probate, and primarily what gives the term "nightmare" to the phrase "nightmare of probate."

> *It's the annual accounting that's the most complex part of probate, and primarily what gives rise to the phrase "nightmare of probate."*

Conceptually, doing an accounting is similar to balancing your check book. Sometimes it balances; sometimes it doesn't. When your checkbook doesn't balance, how much time do you spend trying to figure out where the mistake was made? Often, if it's a small error, you'll decide it's not worth your time to hunt down the error, so you make an adjustment and you move on.

With a probate court accounting, the court will not accept the accounting unless it balances to the penny. Although you balance your check book for just one bank account and one month at a time, a probate accounting typically involves numerous accounts and is for a 12-month period.

Joan spends over 60 hours initially preparing the first accounting for Mary's estate, and when she's done, she finds there's a $3.42 discrepancy. Sadly, she must now go back through all 52 bank statements (12 for the checking account, 12 for the savings account, 12 for the brokerage account, 12 for the money market account, 4 for the Certificate of Deposit) to try to track down the $3.42 error. Did Joan make a math mistake, or did one of the bank's optical scanners make the mistake – misreading a 5 as a 2, or an 8 as a 3? Was it a single mistake or was it actually multiple smaller mistakes? After spending another tortuous 90 hours scrutinizing every bank statement, she finally finds the 2 bank errors and is able to submit the first of many annual accountings she will be filing.

• **The Will War**

Because probate is a court-supervised process, it is very easy for a disgruntled heir to come along and contest a Will. This is exactly what Bill did when he received the legal notice from his sister Joan about his mom having died, and then found out that he was not mentioned in the Will.

Bill didn't even hire a lawyer, since he couldn't afford one. All he did was write a letter, file it at the court house, and ask for a hearing. Joan didn't bother getting a lawyer either, since she figured her mom's Will was very clear in leaving the estate only to Joan and Sam.

At the hearing, the Judge looked at the Will, saw that Bill wasn't mentioned, and decided that Bill was therefore entitled to one-third of his mother's estate. Joan was of course dumbstruck. Why did this happen? Because the law considered Bill to be a "forgotten heir" – the child of a person who has written a Will in which the child is not left anything and is not mentioned at all. After the death of a parent, a forgotten heir has the right to demand the share that he would have received as an heir under the laws of intestacy. The reasoning is that the law presumes the parent either inadvertently forgot the child or incorrectly believed the child was dead, and did not mean to leave him out.

• The Expenses of Probate

The Executor of an estate is either going to spend a lot of time herself doing everything that needs to be done, or else she is going to spend a lot of money hiring an attorney to do it for her. In connection with Mary's estate, after 3 years Joan estimates that she's already spent over 400 hours dealing with the court, dealing with the financial institutions, preparing and filing the required notices, inventory, and accountings, and dealing with her brother's will contest in court. At $25 per hour, which is how much Joan makes as a nurse, she calculates she's spent over $10,000 worth of her time dealing with her mother's probate estate.

The costs associated with probate average around 5% of the estate per year, so for a $500,000 estate, the average costs associated with probate would be $25,000 per year.

Had Joan hired a lawyer to do all of the work, she probably would have spent $10,000 to $15,0000. And these numbers don't even include the various filing fees and probate taxes in connection with probate. Typical estimates for the costs associated with probate put the number at around 5% of the estate per year, so for a $300,000 estate such as Mary's, the average costs associated with probate would be approximately $15,000 per year.

- **Creditor Claims**

Another problem of probate is that creditors typically have a long time (up to five years in Virginia) to file a claim or a lawsuit against the estate, or to go after the beneficiaries of the estate. Joan wasn't worried about creditors because Joan had Mary's Power of Attorney and had been taking care of paying Mary's bills for the past 3 years while Mary was in the nursing home, and Joan "knew" that all of Mary's bills had been paid.

What Joan didn't know was that right after being notified of Mary's death, Joan's brother broke into Mary's house, stole 3 of her credit cards, and charged $45,000 on those cards. Bill also had his girlfriend, pretending to be Joan, call up the credit card companies and change the mailing address on the cards, so Mary never saw the statements come in. Mary had never bothered to cancel the credit cards because she "knew" they had no outstanding balance.

About 15 months passed before the credit card company contacted Joan by phone and told her of the outstanding balance. By then, Joan had distributed almost all of the money from the estate to herself and her two siblings, so the estate didn't have enough money left to pay off the credit cards. Joan figured out what happened and told the credit card company to go after her brother Bill and his girlfriend, which it did, but the credit card company had no luck finding Bill or his girlfriend. So after about another 18 months, the credit card company sued Mary's estate and they also sued Joan and Sam as beneficiaries of the estate since Joan and Sam had already received most of their distributions from the estate. Even though Bill was the one who stole and used the credit cards, Joan and Sam were the ones who got stuck paying.

- **Conclusion**

This case study only deals with *post-mortem* (*i.e.* after-death) probate. Equally onerous is the process of lifetime probate that occurs when someone becomes incapacitated about Mary's story is just one of hundreds of thousands of probate horror stories that occur every day. It provides a summary of the main problems of probate, and why so many people want to avoid it by doing incapacity planning to avoid lifetime probate and by doing estate planning to avoid *post-mortem* probate.

chapter 2

THE PROBLEM OF LONG-TERM CARE

Chapter 1 explained some of the problems associated with probate. Now, let's switch gears and talk about the problem of long-term care.

Whether you're rich, poor, or somewhere in between, you cannot afford to ignore the potentially devastating costs of nursing home care and other types of long-term care.

First of all, what is meant by a long-term care? We're talking about what is also called custodial care, where people need assistance with the activities of daily living – bathing, eating, dressing, going to the bathroom – your basic human needs. Many people needing long-term care also need assistance with the instrumental activities of daily living like cooking, cleaning, taking care of household chores, paying bills, taking care of pets – not quite the basic human needs but pretty essential for someone to be able to live independently on their own. So once people need help with these things, they need long-term care. Of course the degrees of long-term care vary.

> *Whether you're rich, poor, or somewhere in between, you cannot afford to ignore the potentially devastating costs of nursing home care and other types of long-term care.*

A lot of people also need long-term care because of dementia. Almost everybody knows someone with Alzheimer's Disease or some other form of dementia. Alzheimer's Disease is the third leading cause of death in the United States. Of course, before it causes death, it causes people to lose their memory and their ability to handle their own activities of daily living. Some sufferers of Alzheimer's have physical problems; many have no significant physical problems at all, but simply have lost their memory. They have forgotten how to eat and bathe and dress and brush their teeth and do anything to care for themselves. They might be able to do these things with somebody standing next to them and guiding them every step of the way, but they wouldn't do anything if they didn't have constant supervision and reminders.

Nursing homes are the most likely and one of the most expensive creditors that you are likely to face in your lifetime. Consider the following statistics:

- About 70% of Americans who live to age 65 will need long-term care at some time in their lives,[1] over 40% in a nursing home.[2]

- As of 2012, the national average cost of a private room in a nursing home was $248 per day, or $90,520 per year, and the national average cost of a semi-private room was $222 per day, or $81,030 per year. [3]

- On average, someone age 65 today will need some long-term care services for three years. Women need care for longer (on average 3.7 years) than do men (on average 2.2 years). While about one-third of today's 65-year-olds may never need long-term care services, 20 percent of them will need care for more than five years.[4]

---

[1] National Clearinghouse for Long-Term Care Information, http://www.longtermcare.gov at Home > Understanding LTC > Definitions & Need for LTC > Will You Need LTC?

[2] National Clearinghouse for Long-Term Care Information, http://www.longtermcare.gov at at Home > Understanding LTC > Definitions & Need for LTC > Will You Need LTC?

[3] The 2012 MetLife Market Survey of Nursing Home, Assisted Living, Adult Day Services, and Home Care Costs, at http://tinyurl.com/MetLifeSurvey2012.

[4] National Clearinghouse for Long-Term Care Information, http://www.longtermcare.gov at Home > Understanding LTC > Definitions & Need for LTC > How Much Care Will You Need?

- Also, long-term care is not just needed by the elderly. A recent study by Unum Insurance found that 46 percent of its group long-term care claimants were under the age of 65 at the time of disability.[5]

Contrast the above long-term care statistics with statistics for automobile accident claims and homeowner's insurance claims:

- In any given year, an average of only 7.6% of insured vehicle owners file an automobile insurance claim.[6]

- In any given year, an average of only 5.78% of people per year filed a claim on their homeowner's insurance.[7]

Almost everyone who drives has auto insurance, and almost everyone who owns a home has homeowners insurance, yet only about 10% of the population have Long-Term Care Insurance. The other 90% are totally at risk for winding up financially destitute because of the need for nursing home care.

If you're one of the 90% of people who have not purchased long-term care insurance, what are your options for paying for long-term care? The best time for you to address this question is when you do your Estate Planning. It is estimated that only 30% of Americans do estate planning – an absurdly low percentage, but still this is three times greater than the percentage of people who purchase long-term care insurance. The reason you should address the problem of long-term care while doing estate planning is that the best estate plan in the world won't matter a bit if all of

---

[5] Insurance Information Institute,
http://www.iii.org/media/facts/statsbyissue/longtermcare.

[6] Insurance Institute for Highway Safety,
http://www.iihs.org/research/hldi/fact_sheets/CollisionLoss_0910.pdf, based on data from the Highway Loss Data Institute.

[7] Insurance Institute for Highway Safety,
http://www.iii.org/media/facts/statsbyissue/homeowners, based on data from the Insurance Services Office.

your money is wiped out by having to pay privately for nursing home long-term care.

Why do most people wind up financially destitute when needing long-term care? Because of the enormous expense.

The average cost of a nursing home in Northern Virginia (where I live and work) is over $100,000 per year. Some are much higher; right across the street from my office is a nursing home whose minimum fee is $12,000 a month. It's a very good nursing home but it's very expensive.

chapter 3

ARE WILLS THE SOLUTION?

In Chapter 1 we discussed many of the problems of probate – what probate is and why it's such a hassle and why you hear about the nightmares of probate. In Chapter 2 we discussed many of the problems associated with long-term care. Now let's start looking at the possible solutions – starting with Wills.

Is a Last Will and Testament a solution for the problem of probate or the problem of long-term care? The short answer is no. Wills are not the solution for either of these problems. What is a Will? A Will is a legal document. It's signed, witnessed and notarized. It let's you nominate your executor – the one that goes to the court and starts that probate process that we talked about earlier. If you have minor children, it lets you name a guardian for those minor children. A Will is an important legal document, but it has some very serious limitations which most people don't understand.

The biggest drawback of a Will is that it will put your estate through probate. That's the sole purpose of a Will -- it serves as a set of instructions to the probate court, telling the probate court, "here's who I want my assets to go to, here's who I want to be my executor and here's how I want my estate handled." If you don't have a Will when you die, it's called dying "intestate" and your estate will also go through probate. Probate is the exact same process whether you die with a Will or without a Will; it's just that without a Will your estate will be distributed to your legal heirs, subject to the laws of intestacy. As mentioned in Chapter 1, every estate has written simple Will for you. With or without a Will, your assets go through the exact same probate process.

> *The probate process is exactly the same whether you die with a Will or without a Will.*

Another big problem with the Will is it doesn't control all of your assets. Most people think that when they have a Will, it's going to control everything, but it doesn't. We'll talk about why in Chapter 4.

Another problem with a Will is many people use a Will to set up a trust upon their death. It's called a testamentary trust. It takes effect by virtue of the Last Will and Testament. The testamentary trust is simply an extension of probate and in many states, such as Virginia, a testamentary trust is going to prolong the probate process. For instance, if you have a testamentary trust that says "Keep everything in trust for my children until they become age 25" and you have an 11 year old child when you die, your estate would be in probate for 14 years, and your executor would have to file those horrendous annual accountings – the same type we talked about Joan doing in Chapter 1 – every year for 14 years. Talk about a nightmare!

And of course a Will only becomes effective at death. A Will has no effect on your assets while you're alive and certainly does not protect those assets from the expenses of long-term care.

chapter 4

JOINT OWNERSHIP PROBLEMS

Does joint ownership or beneficiary designations help protect assets from probate or long-term care?

Many people attempt to use joint ownership as a sort of inexpensive way to avoid probate. They think they're avoiding probate, and it sometimes works. But what's critical to understand is that joint ownership does not always work as a solution for avoiding probate.

For married couples, you're not avoiding probate, you're just delaying probate until the death of the second spouse.

It's critical to understand that joint ownership does not always work as a solution for avoiding probate.

When you start getting into joint ownership between a parent and a child, you often wind up with lots of problems. Here's an example.

CASE STUDY: PROBLEMS WITH JOINT OWNERSHIP

• **Background**

Priscilla came in to see us a few years ago. She was an 82-year old woman, recently widowed. After her husband died, Priscilla went into her local bank where she had almost all of their assets and various investments, to take her husband's name off of everything. Her oldest daughter, Pam, drove her to the bank because at that point, Priscilla was no longer driving.

The bank executive, trying to be helpful said to Priscilla, "since you're taking your husband's name off these accounts, why don't you add your daughter here to the accounts as a joint owner? That way she can write checks for you to pay your bills if there comes a time when you're not able to do that."

Priscilla thought the bank executive surely knew what he was talking about and so, without legal advice, Priscilla followed his recommendation and added Pam's name as a joint owner on all of Priscilla's accounts.

- **Sometime You Can't Trust In-Laws**

It was about a year later when Priscilla came to see us, telling us that all of her accounts had judgment liens and tax liens on them. The reason for this was some financial trouble that her daughter had gotten into. Except it wasn't even the daughter; it was the daughter's husband.

What happened is that the daughter's husband, Jack, had started a business awhile back. This was a new business, and of course Jack had taken out loans to help fund the new business. And when it came time to sign the loan documents, they always want a personal guarantee and they always want the business-owner's spouse to sign. So Pam signed various documents pledging their house and all of their bank and investment accounts as collateral for the loan.

Well, as happens with so many small businesses, Jack's business failed, and the bank, as well as the IRS (which hadn't been paid some overdue taxes) came calling, got liens against Jack and Pam, and because Pam's name was on all of Priscilla's accounts, all of Priscilla's accounts got attached by these judgments and liens. This was the beginning of an unbelievable nightmare.

- **Sometime You Can't Trust Bank Officers**

The other thing that happened in this case, which Priscilla didn't even realize, is that by adding Pam's name to all of her accounts, she had unintentionally disinherited her other two children. Remember when we said in Chapter 3 that a Will doesn't control all of your assets? This is a perfect example. Priscilla had a Will that said "I leave everything in equal shares to my husband, but if my husband has predeceased me, then to my three children in equal shares."

Sounds simple, right? But it's not, because what Priscilla didn't understand (and what most people don't understand) is that joint ownership takes priority over a Will. The better way to allow someone to pay your bills and help manage your financial affairs is by using a General Power of Attorney, not joint ownership.

When we explained this to Priscilla, she was horrified, and she assured us that she would go to her bank as soon as possible and get this fixed by removing Pam's name as a joint owner and instead giving the bank a copy of the Power of Attorney that we had prepared for Priscilla, wherein she appointed Pam as her Agent to pay her bills and help Priscilla manage her financial affairs.

Sadly, while getting her mail a few days later, Priscilla slipped on the ice and broke her hip. She died the next day during her surgery. Priscilla had not made it back to the bank to remove Pam from her accounts.

- **Sometime You Can't Trust Siblings**

Pam's siblings came to see us a few months after Priscilla's death, having just received the Notice to Heirs from their sister, Pam. They knew they were named equally with Pam in their mom's Will, but Pam had already told them that they wouldn't be receiving any inheritance. According to Pam, their mother "obviously" wanted Pam to inherit everything, because Pam was the one who was providing the most help to Priscilla – taking her to the doctor's appointments, helping around the house, and helping her pay her bills. That's one of the reasons, according to Pam, that Priscilla added Pam's names to her accounts.

Pam's siblings wanted to know what could be done for them to receive what they considered to be their "rightful share" of the estate. According to them, their mother had told them before she died about her meeting with our firm and how she was going to go the bank as soon as possible and remove Pam's name from the accounts so that everything would then pass equally to all three kids through her Will.

Regretfully, we had to tell Pam's siblings that there was really nothing they could do, as joint ownership prevails over the Will. Sure they could hire another attorney and file a lawsuit and try to force Pam to disgorge two-thirds of the estate to them, but we told them that such a lawsuit would likely cost tens of thousands of dollars and they would be very unlikely to win.

MORE PROBLEMS WITH JOINT OWNERSHIP

- **Joint Ownership is Complex and There are Many Types**

Another problem with joint ownership is that the laws of joint ownership are very complex – there are at least four different types of joint ownership, and the laws regarding the meaning and interpretation of these different types of joint ownership vary from state to state. The four most common types of joint ownership are joint tenants with right of survivorship, tenancy by the entirety, community property, and tenancy in common. For some archaic reason the law still uses the word "tenant" instead of "owner." Here's a general explanation of each type of joint ownership.

> *There are at least four different types of joint ownership, and the laws regarding the meaning and interpretation of these different types of joint ownership vary from state to state.*

- **Joint Tenants with Rights of Survivorship**

This type of ownership, sometimes abbreviated as "JTWROS" or "JTROS," means that if one owner dies, the surviving owner or owners will continue to own the asset.

- **Tenancy by the Entirety**

A special type of joint ownership with right of survivorship that is recognized only between married couples, and only in about 18 states, often abbreviated as "TBE" or "T/E." And to make it more complicated, in some of the states where it's allowed, it's only for real estate.

- ## Community Property

A special type of joint ownership recognized only between married couples, and only in only nine states. And some of these states also recognize a type of joint ownership called quasi-community property. Worse yet, there are no two community property states with exactly the same laws on the subject.

- ## Tenancy in Common

When property is owned by two or more people as tenants in common (often abbreviated as "TiC" or "T/C"), each owner is deemed to own a percentage of ownership interest in the property. The percentages don't have to be equal. With tenancy in common, when an owner dies, that owner's share does not pass to the other joint owners, so this type of ownership is also called "joint tenants without right of survivorship."

There are two common problems with joint ownership:

(1) many people title bank accounts and other financial accounts in joint names without knowing whether they are taking ownership as joint tenants with right of survivorship or joint tenants without right of survivorship (tenants in common)

(2) deeds to real estate should always be prepared by an attorney; however, many people purchase real estate, or add owners to real estate, by preparing deeds on their own and simply listing two names as owners, or using the term "joint owners" or "co-owners" without specifying whether the ownership is with or without survivorship.

When this is done, the laws of the state in question will determine what happens to that property when one of the owners dies. The laws of some states presume survivorship. The laws of other states presume no survivorship.

A common problem with property owned by two people as joint tenants without survivorship (tenants in common) is that the asset winds up in probate upon the death of the first co-owner. Worse yet, if the share of the deceased co-owner passes to a minor, or to someone who's disabled or incompetent, it winds up stuck in probate for many years, and can cause lots of other problems too. Here's an example of the problems with joint ownership:

CASE STUDY: MORE JOINT OWNERSHIP PROBLEMS

In an attempt to avoid probate, Fred, a widower, wanted to add his daughter, Janet, to the deed on his home in Virginia. In an attempt to avoid legal fees, Fred prepared the deed himself, based on a sample deed he found online. The deed transferred the house from Fred alone to Fred and Janet as joint owners.

Fred of course assumed that he would die first and that the property would pass to Janet automatically through right of survivorship. He was wrong on both assumptions.

Janet tragically died from cancer just a few years after Fred added her name to the deed, and while Fred was still alive. Instead of Janet's interest passing back to Fred through right of survivorship, Janet's interest passed to her two young twin sons, age 7, because Fred didn't specifically use the words "right of survivorship" in the deed.

Fred didn't even realize that Janet's interest passed to her children until Fred went to sell his house about six months later to move to Florida. Fred (always wanting to save money) put an ad in the paper and stuck a For Sale by Owner sign in his front yard, and started to show house. His house was in great condition and it didn't take him long to find a buyer. The buyer's attorney prepared and presented the contract to Fred and Fred signed it. Planning to use all the money from the sale of his Virginia house to purchase his new house, Fred went ahead and signed a contract for a new house in Florida as soon as he had signed the contract to sell his Virginia house. He scheduled the Florida closing to be 3 days after the closing on the Virginia house.

The day before the closing on the sale of the Virginia house, the closing attorney called up Fred to tell him that the title examiner had just completed the title search, and he noticed that Janet's name was on the deed. The attorney explained to Fred that Janet would need to be at the closing to sign the deed since she was a co-owner. When Fred told the attorney that Janet had died six months earlier, things started to get very complicated.

The attorney explained to Fred that under state law, Janet's interest passed to her young sons when she died because of the way that Fred had worded the deed. Furthermore, because the children were under 18, they could not sign any legal documents; rather, someone would have to go to court to qualify to become the financial guardian for the boys and hold their half of the house, or their half of the sales proceeds, until both children turned 18. During those 11 years, the financial guardian would be subject to court-supervised "living" probate – forced to file annual accountings with the probate court until both children turn 18. And then, at age 18, each child would be entitled to receive his share outright.

Only the financial guardian could sign the closing documents on behalf of the children, so the closing had to be delayed for approximately a month while the father of the boys hired a law firm (that's where we came in) to petition the court to become the boys' financial guardian. During our initial consultation with the boys' father, he told us that one of the twins, Jake, was severely autistic and would probably never be able to live on his own or hold down a job. Based on this fact, we explained that we needed to prepare a special type of Special Needs Trust (called a First-Party SNT or d4A Trust) for the benefit of Jake, and instead of asking to have Jake's share held until age 18, we would ask the court to have his share transferred into the new SNT and held in trust for Jake's entire lifetime, in order to protect the assets of the trust from disqualifying Jake from Medicaid and SSI – two vital public benefits that he would need as an adult. We explained to Jake's father that this SNT needed to have a "payback provision," providing for any balance remaining in the trust at Jake's death to be paid back to the State to reimburse the State for any Medicaid funds that had been used for Jake during his lifetime. We also explained to Jake's dad that this payback provision could have been avoided had Janet done proper estate planning by setting up a Third-Party Special Needs Trust for Jake before she died. Although it was too late to do this for Janet, we did do proper estate planning, including a Third-Party Special Needs Trust, for Jake's dad. (For a more detailed explanation of Special Needs Trusts, please see Chapter 7).

The terrible results of Fred's self-guided attempt to avoid probate were staggering:

(1) Fred literally lost half of the value in his house. It became owned by Janet's children the moment Janet died. Fred never did get any of it back.

(2) You'll recall that Fred was going to use all of his sales proceeds from the Virginia home to purchase the new Florida home. But because Fred lost half the value of his Virginia home, he was no longer able to afford to purchase the Florida home. This resulted in the sellers of the Florida home having to sell that home to a new buyer, and for $45,000 less because the real estate market had taken a nosedive in the meantime. They wound up successfully suing Fred for their loss and Fred was now out another $45,000.

> *The terrible results of Fred's self-guided attempt to avoid probate were staggering.*

(3) Because he was now unable to afford to buy the Florida home, Fred told the buyers of his Virginia home that he was cancelling the contract. But the buyers of his Virginia home were not interested in cancelling the contract; they wanted the house and they had already sold and moved out of their prior home and they had the moving van packed up and were ready to move in. They wound up successfully suing Fred for what's called "specific performance" – forcing him to go through with the sale. They also successfully sued him for all of their monetary damages. Because the closing on the Virginia house had to be delayed for a month, the buyers had to stay in a hotel for a month. They had to pay their moving company for a second complete

move, as well as a month of storage fees, because the moving van had to unpack everything into a storage unit and re-do the entire move a month later. So in addition to being forced to sell the property and become homeless, all the delay cost Fred an extra $18,000 in damages he had to pay the buyers.

(4) While not directly affecting Fred, the father of Janet's sons was not too happy about having to go to court to become financial guardian, or having to file accountings with the probate court every year for 11 years.

EVEN MORE JOINT OWNERSHIP PROBLEMS

Another problem with joint ownership arises when a joint owner becomes disabled. Disabled persons often receive public benefits – Medicaid to pay health care expenses and Supplemental Security Income to help pay bills on a monthly basis. When a disabled person gets money from joint ownership or due to a beneficiary designation, he or she can get disqualified from receiving these vital public benefits.

> *When a disabled person receives money from a beneficiary designation, he or she can get disqualified from vital public benefits.*

chapter 5

PROBLEMS WITH BENEFICIARY DESIGNATIONS

Most people are familiar with beneficiary designations, and many people attempt to use beneficiary designations as an informal way to avoid probate. But, as I'll explain in this chapter, beneficiary designations do not always solve the probate of probate, and can actually cause many more problems than they solve.

WHAT ARE BENEFICIARY DESIGNATIONS?

Some types of assets can be titled with a named beneficiary – someone who is entitled to receive the assets directly after the death of the owner. Insurance policies and retirement plans use the term "beneficiary," but depending on the type of asset involved, a beneficiary designation may be called something different. For example, most banks use the term "POD" (which stands for "Pay on Death") for bank accounts and Certificates of Deposit. The Federal Government uses the term POD for Savings Bonds and other Treasury instruments. Securities (stocks, bonds, and brokerage) accounts typically use the term "TOD," which stands for "Transfer on Death." Regardless of the specific nomenclature used, all beneficiary designations work essentially the same way.

> *Beneficiary designations do not always solve the probate of probate, and can actually cause many more problems than they solve.*

HOW DO BENEFICIARY DESIGNATIONS WORK?

If you're the owner, you retain complete control of your asset while you're alive, and you can change the named beneficiary at any time. After your death, the named beneficiary typically fills out a claim form and files it with the financial institution, along with a Death Certificate showing proof of your death. Upon acceptance of the claim, the idea is that the financial institution distributes the asset to your named beneficiary. This distribution is typically intended to pass directly to the named beneficiary outside of probate but, as we'll see, it doesn't always work out the way it's intended.

PROBLEMS WITH BENEFICIARY DESIGNATIONS

Because of numerous potential problems with beneficiary designations, we don't generally recommend them to my clients as a means to avoid probate. What types of problems have we seen with beneficiary designations?

- **Beneficiary Designations Don't Work for All Types of Assets**

Not all assets can be titled with a beneficiary designation. In most states, cars and real estate can not be owned with a beneficiary designation. Many financial institutions don't offer POD or TOD accounts. Tangible personal property – i.e., home furnishings, jewelry, etc. – is not generally capable of being titled with a beneficiary designation as such items do not generally have any documents of title establishing ownership. Since not all assets can be titled with a beneficiary designation, if you try to avoid probate by using beneficiary designations, some assets will typically still have to go through probate.

- **Beneficiary Designations are Tedious to Change**

There is no single document where you can simply list your assets and declare them "payable on death." To establish a beneficiary designation for each asset, you must fill out a separate beneficiary designation form at the financial institution holding each asset. Every asset that you wish to make "payable on death" has to be individually changed. If you later wish to change your beneficiary designations, you must change each one individually all over again.

- **Beneficiary Designations Don't Work for Minors**

Beneficiary designations should never intentionally be used as a way to distribute assets to minors, because children under the age of 18 are not legally allowed to control assets. If a minor does inherit assets, those assets will have to be held in a court-supervised "living probate" – identical to the probate process described in Chapter 1 – requiring detailed record-keeping, annual accountings, and all the other complications, hassles, and expenses of probate.

- **Beneficiary Designations May Not Work if a Beneficiary Predeceases You**

If a named beneficiary dies before you, that beneficiary's share will typically "lapse," meaning that the share of that beneficiary will go to your estate, and therefore through probate, where it will eventually be distributed under the terms of your Will (if you have one) or under the laws of intestacy for your state of residence.

- **Beneficiary Designations Don't Work for Disabled Beneficiaries**

Beneficiary designations should almost never be used as a way to distribute assets to disabled beneficiaries, for several reasons. First, the inheritance will wind up getting stuck in probate if the disabled beneficiary has been adjudicated to be legally incapacitated and therefore unable to manage assets. Worse, a direct inheritance may disqualify a disabled beneficiary from receiving certain vital public benefits, such as Medicaid and SSI. The proper method for taking care of beneficiary who is disabled is through a Special Needs Trust, as explained in greater detail in Chapter 7.

chapter 6

ESTATE AND INCAPACITY PLANNING

We all know that we will eventually die. At the same time, no one likes to dwell on the prospect of his or her own death. But like everything else in life, failure to plan means planning to fail. If you, your parents, or other loved ones postpone planning until it is too late, you run the risk that your children or other intended beneficiaries — those you love the most — may not receive all that you would hope, or may not be taken care of in the way you would hope. That is what estate planning is all about — making sure that your loved ones are taken care of when you are gone. All adults need to do estate planning — whether you have fifty thousand or five million dollars, you probably want to distribute your assets in a certain way upon your death, which means you need to do estate planning. However, the best estate plan in the world is meaningless if all of your assets wind up being spent on nursing home care before your death, which is why the information in this chapter must be read and understood in light of all the information contained elsewhere in this book.

WHAT IS AN ESTATE?

We should begin a discussion of estate planning with a review of what "estate" and "estate plan" mean.

An "estate" is everything you own: bank accounts, stocks and bonds, real estate, motor vehicles, retirement plans, life insurance, jewelry, household furniture, etc.

An "estate plan," generally, refers to the means by which your estate is passed on to your loved ones on your death. Estate planning can be accomplished through a variety of methods, including:

✓ Revocable Living Trusts

✓ Last Will and Testament / Probate

✓ Lifetime Gifting

✓ Joint Ownership

✓ Beneficiary Designations

✓ Life Estates

Problems often arise when people don't have a coordinated method of passing on their estate. To take just one example, a father's will may say that everything should be equally divided among his children, but if the father creates a joint account with only one of the children, there could be a fight about whether that account go to the should be put back in the pool with the rest of the property or simply go to the child whose name was on the account.

> *An "estate plan," generally, refers to the means by which your estate is passed on to your loved ones on your death.*

THE TWO TYPES OF PROBATE

Without proper incapacity planning documents, your estate will go into living probate if you become incapacitated while you are alive. Dying without a trust, or using a Last Will and Testament as your primary estate planning tool (or dying without a Last Will and Testament), means that your estate will go through *post-mortem* probate upon your death.

The probate process in most states (both for living probate and post-mortem probate) is an unnecessarily complicated, time-consuming, and expensive process, and can go on for many years.

If you become incapacitated while you are alive and you don't have proper Incapacity Planning documents, then someone will have to go to court to have you declared incompetent. This person will seek to become your legal and financial guardian (sometimes the financial guardian is called a conservator).

To initiate the post-mortem probate process in most states, an Executor nominated in a Last Will and Testament must take the original Will and an original death certificate and make at least one appearance at the probate office to officially "qualify" and be "sworn in" as executor. If you died without a Will or Trust, then someone on your behalf goes to the probate office to become the Administrator of your Estate. Both an Executor of a Will and an Administrator of an Estate are called "Personal Representatives" and serve the exact same function.

Once officially appointed, a Guardian/Conservator under a living probate or a Personal Representative under a *post-mortem* probate is accountable to the probate court and is required to prepare and file various legal and financial documents, usually including an initial Inventory of the estate and detailed annual Accountings showing everything coming in to and going out of the estate. Both a Guardian/Conservator and a Personal Representative must see to it that all assets are accounted for and that any valid debts, expenses, and taxes are paid.

> *If you become incapacitated while you are alive and you don't have proper Incapacity Planning documents, then someone will have to go to court to have you declared incompetent.*

Living probate continues for the lifetime of the incapacitated individual. With post-mortem probate, typically after a certain period of time from the date of death, the Personal Representative may distribute the remaining assets of the estate.

INCAPACITY PLANNING

To avoid living probate, you need to have Incapacity Planning documents in place. Incapacity Planning (which can be done by itself or in connection with your Estate Planning) involves the signing of three important documents: (1) a Durable General Power of Attorney for legal and financial affairs; (2) an Advance Medical Directive, which includes a Medical Power of Attorney, Long-Term Care Directive, Living Will, and Post-Mortem Directive; and (3) a Lifestyle Care Plan. Taken together, these three important documents allow you to decide in advance who will manage your legal, personal, and financial affairs in the event of your disability, and exactly how you will be cared for.

Financial Power of Attorney. Just as a living trust avoids *post-mortem* probate, a Durable General Financial Power of Attorney avoids lifetime probate by authorizing your Agent to act on your behalf and sign your name to financial and/or legal documents. The Financial Power of Attorney is an essential tool if you are unable to carry on your legal and financial affairs due to age, illness, or injury. Having a Financial Power of Attorney will generally avoid the need to go through the time-consuming, expensive, and publicly embarrassing guardianship process, which process is subject to probate court supervision. During the guardianship process, someone goes to court to have you declared mentally or physically incompetent and the court appoints one or more persons to serve as your legal guardian and/or conservator – this is the process of living probate.

> *Just as a living trust avoids post-mortem probate, a Durable General Financial Power of Attorney avoids lifetime probate.*

Advance Medical Directive. An Advance Medical Directive (also called a Health Care Power of Attorney or Medical Power of Attorney) authorizes another person (called your "Medical Agent"), to make decisions with respect to your medical care in the event that you are physically or mentally unable to do so, as certified by two physicians. The Advance Medical Directive that we use in our firm is a proprietary document called the Four Needs Advance Directive™ – this document includes four major sections:

1. Medical Power of Attorney	3. Living Will
2. Long-Term Care Directive	4. Post-Mortem Directive

1. A Medical Power of Attorney names someone to make health care decisions for you while you are in a hospital, and someone to give informed consent on your behalf, if you are no longer able;

2. A Long-Term Care Directive allows you to make long-term care decisions for you in case you wind up in a nursing home.

3. The Living Will part of the document deals with end-of life decision making – allowing you to indicate your wishes concerning the use of artificial or extraordinary measures to prolong your life artificially in the event of a terminal illness or injury.

4. The Post-Mortem Directive covers issues such as disposition of bodily remains, organ donation, and funeral arrangements.

Lifestyle Care Plan. A Lifestyle Care Plan is a document that is created by special software that gathers, organizes, stores and disseminates information provided by you in an interview, in order to better serve your future healthcare needs and to guide those who you will depend or for future care. The Lifestyle Care Plan identifies your specific needs, desires, habits and preferences and guides your caregiver in a unique manner. See page ? for a detailed example of the tremendous benefits of a Lifestyle Care Plan.

ESTATE PLANNING

A well-crafted estate plan could permit your family to save potentially tens or even hundreds of thousands of dollars on taxes, court costs and attorneys' fees. Most importantly, it affords the comfort that your loved ones can mourn your loss without being simultaneously burdened with unnecessary red tape and financial confusion.

Estate planning (including the decision as to whether to use a Will or a Living Trust as your primary estate planning tool), is vitally important for someone who may soon be entering a nursing home.

Just as a good incapacity plan avoids lifetime probate, a good estate plan – one that uses a Revocable Living Trust as the primary estate planning tool – avoids post-mortem probate.

REVOCABLE LIVING TRUSTS

A trust is a legal entity which is capable of owning financial assets, real estate, and/or other property.

A living trust is a trust that comes into existence during your lifetime, and a Revocable Living Trust is simply a living trust that can be revoked or modified during your lifetime, as opposed to some living trusts that are irrevocable. Using a fully-funded Revocable Living Trust as your primary estate planning tool means that your estate will not go through probate after your death. You create a Revocable Living Trust by signing a contractual document called a "Declaration of Trust" or "Trust Agreement." You are typically the trustee of your own living trust until your death. If you are the initial

> *Most people use a Revocable Living Trust as their primary estate planning tool in order to make things easier for their trusted loved ones by avoiding the time and complications of post mortem probate.*

trustee, then upon your death or disability, a successor trustee whom you have named takes over as trustee of the trust and, after paying any valid debts, expenses, and taxes, distributes the trust assets to or for the benefit of your named beneficiaries or, if called for in the trust, continues to hold the trust assets until the occurrence of a predetermined event.

The main feature of a Revocable Living Trust is that the trustee is not accountable to the court, and therefore not subject to probate. Most people therefore use a Revocable Living Trust as their primary estate planning tool in order to make things easier for their trusted loved ones by avoiding the time and complications of probate. There are also some advantages of using a Revocable Living Trust to consolidate your assets and simplify your finances while you're alive.

chapter 7

SPECIAL NEEDS PLANNING

Special Needs Planning means legal and financial planning that is done for the benefit of a person with special needs. The primary goal of Special Needs Planning is to protect the quality of life of the person with special needs. Money that is legally protected through proper Special Needs Planning can be used to provide a person with special needs enhanced care and a better quality of life while still receiving vital public benefits such as SSI and Medicaid.

> *The primary goal of Special Needs Planning is to protect the quality of life of the person with special needs.*

Special Needs Planning is done in a multitude of situations, including: Estate Planning by parents with a special needs child; an individual with special needs coming into an inheritance or settling a personal injury claim; or a spouse planning for a disabled spouse.

This chapter will provide a brief introduction and overview of the different types of Special Needs Planning to assist parents and other relatives of persons with special needs.

SPECIAL NEEDS ESTATE PLANNING

Parents of children with special needs face unique estate planning concerns:

• How do you leave funds for your child without causing the child to lose vital public benefits?

• How do you ensure that the funds are well-managed

• How do you ensure that your other children are not over-burdened with caring for their sibling?

- What is a fair way to divide your estate?

- How do you ensure there's enough money to meet your disabled child's needs?

Parents of special needs children often try to resolve these concerns by leaving the special needs child's share to one of the healthy children, disinheriting the child with special needs. Parents who choose this approach may have been told, incorrectly, that their special needs child can't inherit anything because he will lose his public benefits. Parents may also mistakenly think that their child won't need an inheritance because he'll be taken care of by public benefits. This type of planning also assumes that the healthy child will in fact use the money to take care of the special needs sibling.

The approach of disinheriting your special needs child is generally discouraged for a number of reasons. First, public benefits programs are often inadequate to provide complete support and assistance for a person with special needs. Public benefits need to be supplemented with other resources in order to provide optimal care. Second, both public benefits programs and individual circumstances change over time; what's working today may not work tomorrow, so other resources need to be available. Third, relying on a healthy child to take care of a special needs sibling may place an undue burden on the healthy children and can strain relations between them. It makes it unclear whether inherited money belongs to the healthy child to spend as he pleases, or whether he must set it aside for his special needs sibling. If one child sets money aside, and the other doesn't, resentments can build that may split the family forever. When money is used by a healthy child to take care of a special needs sibling, this may trigger gift consequences and create tax and public benefit concerns.

The better solution to all of these problems is a special type of trust called a "Special Needs Trust." Such trusts, also called "Supplemental Needs Trusts," fulfill two primary functions: the first is to manage funds for someone who may not be able to do so himself or herself due to disability. The second is to preserve the beneficiary's eligibility for public benefits, whether that be Medicaid, Supplemental Security Income, public housing, or any other program.

WHAT IS A SPECIAL NEEDS TRUST?

First, a short explanation of what trusts are and how they work: a trust is a form of ownership of property, whether real estate or investments, where one person – the trustee – manages such property for the benefit of someone else – the beneficiary. The trustee must follow the instructions laid out in the trust agreement as to how to spend the trust funds on the beneficiary's behalf – whether and when to distribute the trust income and principal. In the special needs context, trusts fall generally into two main categories: Third-Party SNTs that one person creates and funds for the benefit of someone else, and First-Party SNTs (also called d4a trusts) that are created for the person with special needs using that person's own money.

THIRD-PARTY SPECIAL NEEDS TRUSTS

A trust that is created and funded by someone for the benefit of a person with special needs is often called a "third party SNT." This type of trust can be created while you are alive by using a revocable or irrevocable living trust, or can be created upon your death through your living trust or through your Last Will and Testament. If you create and fund a third-party SNT during your lifetime, you can place assets into the SNT while you are alive and/or upon your death. This type of third-party SNT can also be used to receive any inheritance that may come from a grandparent or other family member, provided the other family member properly names the SNT that you created. Because the SNT will own the assets, the beneficiary will not become ineligible for government benefits. On the contrary, the SNT allows the beneficiary to receive vital public benefits, while the funds in the SNT can be used for the

A Special Needs Trust preserves the beneficiary's eligibility for public benefits such as Medicaid and SSI.

special needs beneficiary to improve care and quality of life until his or her own death, at which time any assets left in trust can pass to whoever you name in the trust document.

To determine the exact provisions to include in an SNT, a parent should work with a qualified Elder Law and Special Needs Planning Attorney. Your attorney will consider information about you and your disabled beneficiary and how you want the trust funds used. Your attorney will base his or her recommendation on your beneficiary's age, what benefits your beneficiary is receiving or is likely to receive in the future, the eligibility requirements for benefits, and the kind and amount of assets you plan to place in the trust.

FIRST-PARTY SPECIAL NEEDS TRUSTS

The above discussion involves estate planning by parents for money they plan to leave their child with special needs. However, a third-party special needs trust cannot hold funds belonging to the disabled individual himself. Unexpected events may trigger money being paid directly to a person with special needs. This may happen, for example, through an inheritance from a family member, life insurance proceeds, or a personal injury settlement. If a person is about to receive money or property in an amount that will cause him or her lose benefits, a First-Party SNT – often called a "(d)(4)(A)" trust, so-named after the U.S. Code section that authorizes this type of trust – is a planning option that can help set aside some or all of the money for supplemental needs and still allow the person to stay on public benefits without any period of disqualification. If a person has already received money or property in an amount that has caused him or her lose benefits, the First-Party SNT can still be used as a tool to set aside some or all of the money for supplemental needs and allow the person to re-obtain public benefits.

A (d)(4)(A) trust must be created while the disabled individual is under age 65 and must be established by his or her parent, grandparent, legal guardian, or by a court. A (d)(4)(A) trust also must provide that at the beneficiary's death any remaining trust funds will first be used to reimburse the state for Medicaid paid on the beneficiary's behalf. Because of this payback provision, this type of trust is sometimes called a "payback trust." The state must approve all payback trusts to make sure that they meet the standards in the law. After the state is paid back, any assets left in the trust can pass to the people chosen by the grantor and named in the trust instrument.

CHOOSING THE SPECIAL NEEDS TRUSTEE

Choosing a trustee is one of the most difficult parts of planning for a person with special needs. The trustee of a special needs trust must be able to fulfill all of the normal functions of a trustee – accounting, investments, tax returns and distributions – and also be able to meet the needs of the special beneficiary. The latter often means having an understanding of the various public benefits programs, having sensitivity to the needs of the beneficiary, and having knowledge of special services that may be available. There are a number of possible solutions, including professional trustees such as banks, trust companies, and law firms who work with special needs trust.

> *The Trustee of a Special Needs Trust should have an understanding of public benefits programs, sensitivity to the needs of the beneficiary, and knowledge of special services that may be available.*

Often parents choose to appoint co-trustees – for example a trust company or law firm as a professional trustee along with a healthy child as a family trustee. Working together, the co-trustees can provide the necessary experience to meet the needs of the child with special needs. Unfortunately, in many cases such a combination is not available. Some professional trustees require a minimum amount of funds in the trust. In other situations, there is no appropriate family member to appoint as a co-trustee.

Where the size of the trust is insufficient to justify hiring a professional trustee, two other solutions are possible. The first option is simply to have a family member trustee who would hire accountants, attorneys and investment advisors to help with administering the trust. Where no appropriate family member is available to serve as co-trustee, the parent may direct the professional trustee to consult with specific individuals who know and can care for the child with special needs. These could be family members who are not appropriate trustees, but who can serve in an advisory role. Or they may be social workers or care managers or others who have both personal and professional knowledge of the beneficiary. This role may be formalized in the trust document as a "Care Committee" or "Advisory Committee." The second option is to use a pooled trust.

WHEN TO USE POOLED SPECIAL NEEDS TRUSTS

A pooled SNT is a special type of SNT that is created by a nonprofit organization. The nonprofit organization may act as the trustee of the pooled SNT, or it may select the trustee. Individuals have separate accounts in the pooled SNT, but all the money is pooled together and invested by the trustee. Individual beneficiaries get the services of a professional trustee and more investment options because there is more money overall. A third-party pooled trust provides a way to benefit from a special needs trust without having to create one yourself.

Just as with single-beneficiary trusts discussed above, there are both "third-party" pooled SNTs (which you can use to give money during life, or leave money upon death, for a special needs beneficiary) and "first-party" pooled SNTs – also called "(d)(4)(C)" trusts – used to protect money that belongs to the special needs beneficiary. Unlike the individual payback trust – i.e., the (d)(4)(A) discussed above, which may be created only for those under age 65 – pooled SNTs may be for beneficiaries of any age and may be created by the beneficiary himself. In addition, at the beneficiary's death the state does not have to be repaid for Medicaid expenses so long as the funds are retained in the trust for the benefit of other disabled beneficiaries. Although a pooled trust is an option for a disabled individual over age 65 who is receiving Medicaid or SSI, those over age 65 who make transfers to this type of trust may incur a transfer penalty.

Funding The Third-Party Special Needs Trust

As a parent or guardian, you want to ensure that your child with special needs will remain financially secure even when you are no longer there to provide support. Given the significant, ongoing expenses involved in your child's care and uncertainty about what needs may arise after you are gone or what public benefits may be available, determining how much a special needs trust (SNT) should hold is no small feat.

Fortunately, help in calculating your "special needs goal" is available from financial planners with expertise in disability issues, as well as from special needs calculators, which are accessible free of charge on the Internet. There are two such calculators available on the Web:

> **MetDesk Special Needs Calculator at:**
> http://tinyurl.com/MetDesk-SNT-Calculator
>
> **Merrill Lynch Special Needs Calculator at:**
> http://tinyurl.com/Merrill-SNT-Calculator

Using one of these calculators, either on your own or with the help of an advisor, is an excellent way to begin making concrete plans for your child's future. Based on information you provide about anticipated income and expenses, the calculators offer a realistic estimate of how much your child will need in lifetime financial support. Financial planners suggest running this type of calculation periodically, particularly as your child nears adulthood, to ensure the estimate reflects the most accurate, up-to-date information about needs and circumstances.

- **Getting Started with Funding**

The first step in determining the amount you must set aside in an SNT is to consider your goals and your expectations for your child's future. If you haven't yet created a Letter of Intent or an

Advance Care Plan for your child, this is the time to draft such a document. The Letter of Intent or Advance Care Plan should address factors such as your child's medical condition, guardianship needs, ability to work and desired living arrangements, all of which will drive your special needs calculation.

Once you've considered the "big picture," you'll need to identify your child's future income sources and living expenses. The online calculators identify relevant categories for you (e.g., public benefits income. transportation costs).

Next, you'll need to tackle the most arduous part of the process, placing a dollar value on each category. You can start by listing any current income or expenses likely to continue into your child's adult years. You'll need to consider income from sources such as life insurance proceeds, gifts, inheritances, and legal settlements, as well as from employment and public benefits such as Supplemental Security Income and Social Security Disability Income.

On the expenses side of the column, broad categories include, but are not necessarily limited to:

- Housing: rent, a mortgage, utilities, insurance, taxes, maintenance.

- Transportation: car payments, auto insurance, fuel, repairs, public transportation costs.

- Medical care: doctor visits, therapy, prescription drugs.

- Care assistance: respite, custodial, nursing home care.

- Special equipment: wheelchairs, assistive technologies, durable medical equipment, computers, service animals.

- Personal needs: grooming, hobbies, entertainment, vacations.

- Education and employment costs: tuition, books, supplies, tutoring.

- Future asset replacement costs: for a car, major appliances, electronics, furnishings.

- **Running the Funding Calculation**

Prior to running the calculation, you may need to indicate your child's life expectancy and the number of years remaining until your retirement. Once you've input all required data, the calculator automatically will run an analysis of your funding needs based on preset assumptions about the rate of inflation and your after-tax investment returns. Both calculators indicate the amount of annual savings required to meet your goal. The Merrill Lynch calculation includes a lump-sum savings goal that must be met by retirement, as well as a year-by-year cash-flow analysis indicating any shortfalls or surpluses for a given year.

- **Considering the Funding "What Ifs"**

Financial planners advise that running alternative calculations can help you plan adequately for worst- and best-case scenarios. One variable to consider is your child's ability to earn income. For example, if he or she is able to work more than expected, earned income may cover more expenses, but SSI payments will likely be reduced. As your child's disability advances, he or she may need to leave the workforce, potentially increasing SSI payments but also adding new expenses.

Another critical factor is the impact of higher or lower investment returns on the amount you must set aside. If your child is very young, you may plan to invest aggressively, pursuing a higher rate of return than if he were nearing adulthood. The reason "an investment rule of thumb" is that you generally can take somewhat greater risks with a longer-term investment because you have more time to recover from dips in the market. If you anticipate a lower rate of return for any reason, you will need to compensate by setting aside more in savings.

As you can see, to some extent this is more of an art than a science. You can make your best guess or work with a financial planner who specializes in this field and who can bring to bear her experience with many families in similar situations.

- **Finding the Funds – Using Life Insurance**

Once you have a realistic estimate in hand, you'll need to consider how to fund this need without sacrificing such financial goals as college for your other children and retirement for yourselves. You also need to balance the needs of your special needs child with your wish to benefit your other children, as well as cover your current expenses. You may not be able to completely fund the dollar amount resulting from the above calculations, but having a target can assist your planning.

Many parents find that a second-to-die life insurance policy is the easiest option to fund an SNT because the premiums are often

> *Many parents find that a second-to-die life insurance policy is the easiest option to fund an SNT because the premiums are often lower. However, a joint first-to-die policy might make also make sense for many parents.*

lower. However, a joint first-to-die policy might make more sense for many parents, especially if one parent is the primary wage earner and one parent is the primary caregiver for the disabled child. With a first-to-die policy, if the wage-earner parent dies first, the policy will provide funds needed for the caregiver parent to be able to continue providing the care; if the caregiver parent dies first, the policy will provide funds needed for the wage-earner parent to hire a replacement caregiver.

- **Conclusion About Funding an SNT**

In short, how much you fund your SNT and how large an insurance policy to purchase will be a question of balance among your current needs, your retirement funding, the needs of your other children, if any, and the anticipated needs of your special needs child.

Finally, be sure to create or update your estate plan and determine which of your assets you'll leave to the SNT. Also advise relatives of the need to direct gifts and bequests to the SNT, rather than the child, to avoid the risk of disqualifying the child from eligibility for public benefits.

chapter **8**

HOW TO PAY FOR NURSING HOME CARE

One of greatest concerns people have about nursing home care is how to pay for it. There are basically four ways to pay for the cost of the care provided by a nursing home:

Private Pay. This is the method many people must use at first. It means paying for the cost of a nursing home out of your own pocket. Unfortunately, with nursing home bills of more than $12,000 per month at some facilities, few people can afford to pay on their own for a long-term stay in a nursing home. Even those who can afford to do so often desire to explore other options — options that allow them to retain some or all of their assets for other important needs, while still permitting them to pay for nursing home care.

Long-Term Care Insurance. If you have long-term care insurance coverage, this could help pay the costs of needed home care or nursing home care. Unfortunately, only about ten percent of the population carry long-term care insurance, so most people facing a nursing home stay do not have this type of coverage in place. Many people who would like to purchase this type of coverage find that they can not afford it. How to purchase the best long-term care policy is a complicated subject that is well-worth exploring if you

> *Long-Term Care Insurance should be given serious consideration if it is affordable for you, especially in view of the federally-mandated Long-Term Care Partnership, which encourages you to use long-term care insurance as a type of Medicaid Asset Protection.*

are in your 50s or 60s and still healthy. It should be given serious consideration if it is affordable for you, especially in view of the new federally-mandated "Long-Term Care Partnership," which allows you to use long-term care insurance as a type of Medicaid Asset Protection – to protect an amount of assets equivalent to the premium paid for the insurance. If you are thinking about purchasing a long-term care insurance policy, an experienced elder law attorney can assist you in finding the best policy by helping you compare and contrast the numerous types of policies available and the different types and levels of coverage offered, as well as the independent ratings and financial stability of the insurance company providing the coverage. You should also discuss with an elder law attorney some of the uses of, and alternatives to, long-term care insurance, so that you have a better understanding of the cost versus benefit of such coverage. You will find additional information about Long-Term Care Insurance starting on page 61.

Department of Veterans Affairs. The Department of Veterans Affairs (VA) primarily pays for long-term care through the Veterans "Aid and Attendance" Special Pension Benefit payments. In some parts of the country, there are also nursing homes that are run by the Department of Veterans Affairs. You will find additional information about the Veterans "Aid and Attendance" Special Pension starting on page 69.

Medicaid. This is a combined federally-funded and state-funded benefit program, administered by each state, that can pay for the cost of a nursing home if certain asset and income tests are met. According to AARP, about 70 percent of nursing home residents are supported, at least in part, by Medicaid. Medicaid qualification and eligibility will be discussed in greater detail starting on page 75.

A WORD ABOUT MEDICARE

You will notice that Medicare is NOT listed among the sources of funds used to pay for long-term care in a nursing home. This is because Medicare does not pay a penny for long-term care, ever. Medicare is the national health insurance program primarily for people 65 years of age and older, those under age 65 who have been disabled for at least 24 months, and people with kidney failure. Medicare may provide some coverage for short-term (up to 100 days) rehabilitation in a nursing facility, provided you continue to get better from the rehabilitation, but you must meet certain strict qualification rules, which will be discussed in greater detail starting on page 55.

> *Medicare Does Not Ever Pay a Penny for Long-term Care. Medicare Often Pays for Short-Term Rehab that Takes Place in a Nursing Home, but that is NOT Long-term Care.*

chapter 9

WHAT DOES MEDICARE COVER?

Most people have a great deal of confusion between Medicare and Medicaid.

Medicare is a federally-funded and federally-administered health insurance program, primarily designed for individuals over age 65. Medicare does not cover long-term care under any circumstances.

If you are enrolled in a traditional Medicare plan, and you've been in the hospital at least three days, and you are admitted directly from the hospital into a rehab facility (which are typically skilled nursing facilities) for short-term rehabilitation (i.e., therapy and treatment designed to make you better), then Medicare should pay the full cost of this short-term rehab stay for the first 20 days, and may continue to pay part of the cost of the short-term rehab stay for the next 80 days — with a per day deductible that you must pay privately (although there are Medicare supplement insurance policies that sometimes cover that deductible). There is also a Medicare Managed Care Plan, for which the 3-day hospital stay may not be required, and for which the deductible for days 21 through 100 is waived, provided certain strict qualifying rules are met. But whether the plan

> *It is important to understand that Medicare does not pay at all for long-term care.*

is traditional Medicare or Medicare Managed Care (MMC), the nursing home resident must be receiving daily rehabilitative care and must be improving. Medicare does not pay for long-term care, *i.e.*, for custodial nursing home stays or in-home care.

In a best case scenario, traditional Medicare or MMC will provide some coverage for the hospital stay and rehabilitation of up to 100 days for each "spell of illness" (although in our experience coverage usually falls far short of the 100-day maximum). If you recover sufficiently that you do not require a Medicare-covered care benefit for 60 consecutive days, you may be eligible for another benefit period, i.e., another 100 days of Medicare coverage, but the illness or disorder must not be a chronic degenerative condition from which you will not recover.

What happens if you've used up the 100 days of coverage and still need more rehabilitation, or if you need to move into long-term nursing home care? You're back to one of the alternatives outlined above: long-term care insurance, paying the bills with your own assets, or qualifying for Medicaid.

chapter 10

WHY MEDICAID PLANNING IS ETHICAL

Medicaid Asset Protection is absolutely ethical and moral; in fact, it is the "right" thing to do if a family is concerned about the long-term care of a loved one. From a moral and ethical standpoint, Medicaid planning is no different from income tax planning and estate planning.

JUST LIKE INCOME TAX PLANNING

Income tax planning involves trying to find all of the proper and legal deductions, credits, and other tax savings that you are entitled to — taking maximum advantage of existing laws. Income tax planning also involves investing in tax-free bonds, retirement plans, or other tax-favored investment vehicles, all in an effort to minimize what you pay in income taxes and maximize the amount of money that remains in your control to be used to benefit you and your family.

JUST LIKE ESTATE PLANNING

Estate planning involves trying to plan your estate to minimize the amount of estate taxes and probate taxes that your estate will have to pay to the government, again taking maximum advantage of the existing laws. Similar to income-tax planning, estate planning is a way to minimize what your estate pays in taxes

> *Congress accepts the realities of Medicaid Planning . . . planning ahead to accelerate qualification for Medicaid is no different than maximizing your income tax deductions to receive the largest income tax refund allowable.*

and maximize the amount of money that remains in your estate to be used to benefit your family.

Similarly, Medicaid planning involves trying to find the best methods to transfer, shelter, and protect your assets in ways that take maximum advantage of existing laws, all in an effort to minimize what you pay and maximize the amount of money that remains in your control to be used to benefit you and your family.

Like income-tax planning and estate planning, Medicaid planning requires a great deal of extremely complex knowledge due in part to constantly-changing laws, so you need to work with an experienced elder law attorney who knows the rules and can advise you properly.

JUST LIKE LONG-TERM CARE INSURANCE

For seniors over the age of 65, Medicaid has become equivalent to federally-subsidized long-term care insurance, just as Medicare is equivalent to federally-subsidized health insurance. Congress accepts the realities of Medicaid Planning through rules that protect spouses of nursing home residents, allow Medicaid Asset Protection via the purchase of qualified Long-Term Care Insurance policies, allow the exemption of certain types of assets, and permit individuals to qualify even after transferring assets to a spouse or to a disabled family members or to a caregiver child. To plan ahead and accelerate qualification for Medicaid is no different than planning to maximize your income tax deductions to receive the largest income tax refund allowable. It's no different than taking advantage of tax-free municipal bonds. It's no different than planning your estate to avoid paying estate taxes.

> *The ways that Elder Law attorneys are able to shelter and protect assets may seem like "magic" to you, but that's only because you don't possess our legal knowledge and experience.*

JUST LIKE MAGIC

The "magic" that Elder Law attorneys are able to perform is not based on slight of hand. Elder Law attorneys do not "hide" assets.

On the contrary, we provide total disclosure of everything we do to the relevant Medicaid agencies when we file the Medicaid application, as failure to provide full disclosure of all assets and all transfers would be a federal crime. The ways that Elder Law attorneys are able to shelter and protect assets may seem like "magic" to you, but that's only because you don't possess our legal knowledge and experience. It's the same with magicians -- the magic only appears to be "magical" because you don't know how the trick is done. Just as magicians study and train for years to become good magicians, Elder Law attorneys also study and train for years to become experts in our field. To become a Certified Elder Law Attorney, attorneys must: spend an average of at least 16 hours per week practicing elder law during the three years preceding their application; must handle a minimum of 60 elder law matters, in 13 different areas of elder law, during those three years; participate in at least 45 hours of continuing legal education in elder law during the preceding three years; submit five references from attorneys familiar with

Is it an ethical social policy that provides full coverage for most diseases but forces those with certain conditions to become impoverished in order to gain access to the basic care that they need to survive?

their competence and qualifications in elder law; and must pass a full-day certification examination (one of the most recent exams had a 19% pass rate). Done with respect for the law and compassion for the elders that are being protected, Medicaid planning is not only ethically justified -- it is often imperative to the individual's quality of life.

MEDICAID ASSET PROTECTION IS NEEDED BECAUSE OUR HEALTH CARE SYSTEM IS DISCRIMINATORY

Within the United States, no one yet has a right to basic long-term care. We give seniors virtually universal coverage for certain types of health problems. Treatment and surgery for health conditions such as heart disease, lung disease, kidney disease, bone disease, cancer, and hundreds of other medical conditions will not impoverish most seniors because Medicare and private health insurance cover these diseases, and we all pay our fair share for such coverage. But neither Medicare nor private health insurance cover chronic illnesses such as Alzheimer's disease or other type of brain diseases causing dementia or loss of the ability to function independently. For these types of diseases, seniors must become officially "impoverished" under federal and state Medicaid rules in order to gain access to basic long-term care. Is this an ethical social policy that arbitrarily distinguishes among these different types of diseases? Is this an ethical social policy that provides full coverage for most diseases but forces elders with certain conditions to become impoverished in order to gain access to basic long-term care? Is it a surprise to anyone that most seniors will want to look for legal ways to preserve the efforts of their lifetime in order to protect themselves from this unfair and arbitrary social policy? Medicaid planning is not about "cheating" or "gaming" the system; it is about preserving a client's dignity and self-worth in the face of an unfair and arbitrary social policy. The ethical scandal is America's public policy, not the desire of seniors to avoid poverty.

chapter 11

LONG-TERM CARE INSURANCE

Long-term care insurance, one of many types of long-term care asset protection, can be a good way for some people to protect assets for future long-term care needs. You pay a theoretically modest premium to the insurance company in exchange for the insurance company paying for your long-term care needs in the future. Long-term care insurance coverage could help pay the costs of needed nursing home care. Unfortunately, only about ten percent of the population carry long-term care insurance, so most people facing a nursing home stay do not have this type of coverage in place. Many people who would like to purchase this type of coverage find that they can not afford it.

However, this type of insurance coverage is worth exploring if you are under age 65 and still healthy, especially in view of the federally-mandated "Long-Term Care Partnership," which allows you to use special long-term care insurance for Medicaid Asset Protection – to protect an amount of assets equivalent to the total amount of insurance coverage you purchase.

If you are thinking about purchasing a long-term care insurance policy, an experienced, independent insurance agent who specializes in long-term care insurance can assist you in finding the best policy by helping you compare and contrast the numerous types of policies available and the different types and levels of coverage offered, as well as the independent ratings and financial stability of the insurance company providing the coverage. Consideration should be given to purchasing a long-term care insurance policy that covers home

> *Elder law attorneys are uniquely qualified to assess and address all of the issues that a client needing long-term care will face.*

care only, as nursing home care can be paid for with Medicaid through proper Medicaid Asset Protection discussed later starting on page 75.

Additionally, you should discuss with a qualified elder law attorney some of the alternatives to long-term care insurance, so that you have a better understanding of the cost versus benefit of such coverage. Elder law attorneys are uniquely qualified to assess and address all of the issues that a client needing long-term care will face. Most insurance agents do not have a complete understanding of nursing home laws and Medicaid laws, and are usually not able to adequately address all of the issues surrounding long-term care.

WHAT ELDER LAW ISSUES MUST BE CONSIDERED WHEN PURCHASING LONG-TERM CARE INSURANCE?

When shopping for a long-term care insurance policy, it is crucial to consider carefully the entire financial situation of both spouses and to consider the possible alternative of not purchasing long-term care insurance. Failure to do so can result in purchasing too little coverage, too much coverage, or coverage for the wrong spouse, each of which can actually be worse than purchasing no coverage at all.

EXAMPLE OF PURCHASING TOO LITTLE COVERAGE

Consider Joe and Linda, a married couple facing Joe's nursing home costs of $8,500 per month. Joe has $4,000 in monthly retirement income, as well as a long-term care insurance policy with a monthly benefit of $4,500 (based on a daily benefit of $150). Linda's only income is Social Security of $700 per month. At first glance, the couple seems better off with the long-term care policy; they have an extra $4,500 per month, without which they could not afford the nursing home. With the insurance, Joe has exactly enough income to pay the private rate of the nursing home. Unfortunately, Linda's monthly expenses, even with Joe in the nursing home, are approximately $2,200 per month, and Joe is not eligible for Medicaid assistance because his income (including the long-term care insurance benefit) is sufficient to pay the private nursing home bill.

In this example, Joe's long-term care insurance policy does not provide enough of a benefit to allow Linda to have sufficient income to meet her needs. If Joe's long-term care insurance policy had provided a $6,000 monthly benefit ($200 per day instead of $150), then Joe would have income of $10,000 per month and $1,500 of Joe's retirement income would be available for Linda's monthly expenses. Joe's extra $1,500 per month plus Linda's own $700 per month would be just enough income for Linda to live on. Joe and Linda could have fully financed Joe's long-term care needs and ensured that Linda would have enough funds to meet her monthly expenses.

If Joe and Linda had recognized this shortfall and decided to not purchase the long-term care insurance, or if they could not afford the increased premiums for the increased monthly benefit, they could instead use Medicaid assistance to help pay for Joe's nursing home costs. Most of Joe's $4,000 per month of income would normally be required to pay the nursing home expenses; Linda would keep her $700 per month. However, because Linda's income is so low, the Medicaid rules would allow Linda to receive part of Joe's income to help her with her monthly living expenses. Linda could receive a monthly maintenance needs allowance of up to $2,898[8] (including her income) which includes allowances for housing and utilities. Therefore, in this case, Joe and Linda would have the nursing home costs paid, and Linda would have up to $2,898 monthly for her support.

> *If Joe and Linda had recognized this shortfall and decided to not purchase the long-term care insurance, or if they could not afford the increased premiums for the increased monthly benefit, they could instead use Medicaid assistance to help pay for Joe's nursing home costs.*

[8]This is the maximum monthly maintenance needs allowance as of January 1, 2013.

The bottom line? Either buy enough long-term care insurance coverage or don't buy any. It doesn't make sense to pay insurance premiums and then be bankrupted by nursing home fees anyway because of insufficient coverage. And if you do buy coverage, be sure to get adequate inflation coverage. As with other medical expenses, the inflation rate in nursing home fees is currently quite high. In 10 years, the cost of the nursing homes, at the current rate of inflation, will be about twice what it is today.

WHICH SPOUSE SHOULD GET COVERAGE?

Often a married couple will be able to afford coverage for only one spouse. Statistics alone would dictate that the wife should purchase the policy, as women tend to live longer than men are therefore more likely than men to end up in a nursing home for a long period of time. However, this is often the wrong answer! For a couple where the husband's retirement income is much higher than the wife's retirement income, it is actually much more important to purchase coverage for the husband. As just explained, if the husband enters the nursing without adequate long-term care coverage, the wife may wind up destitute or without sufficient income to live on.

The other half of the story is what happens if the wife goes into the nursing home first. Using the same fact scenario, let's now assume that Linda enters the nursing home first and does not have long-term care coverage. Is there any problem? No, not at all, because we can get Linda's nursing home paid for almost entirely through Medicaid assistance. Linda's $700 monthly income would have to go to the nursing home, but Medicaid will pay the rest. Joe will be able to keep 100% of his retirement income and, with proper Medicaid Asset Protection Planning, will be able to keep all of his assets.

> *For a couple where the husband's retirement income is much higher than the wife's retirement income, it is actually much more beneficial to purchase long-term care insurance for the husband.*

How Much Coverage Do You Need?

We don't recommend anyone purchasing more than five years of long-term care insurance coverage. For one reason, the average nursing home stay is only approximately 3 years. Secondly, after moving to a nursing home, your family can commence the process of Medicaid Asset Protection, which is the primary focus of my practice as and Elder Law attorney. Using Medicaid Asset Protection, we can have you transfer your assets into a special type of asset protection trust. After five years have passed, if you are still alive, you'll be able to qualify for Medicaid to pay your nursing home costs (provided the assets remaining in your name do not exceed Medicaid's limits). Using this strategy, you'll only need long-term care coverage only for five years before Medicaid coverage commences, so there's no need to purchase more than five years of long-term care coverage.

How Do You Know If You Can Afford Long-Term Care Insurance?

You should generally only purchase long-term care insurance if you can pay the premiums out of your disposable income, i.e, if the premiums are affordable using income that you would otherwise add to your savings.

How Can You Reduce Your Premium?

There are five ways to reduce the cost of Long-term Care Insurance. First, request a one-hundred day elimination period since Medicare may pay some or all of the first hundred days (to the extent skilled nursing care is required). Second, the daily benefit purchased can be reduced by income from pensions and Social Security, to the extent these items may not be needed by a spouse. Third, the benefit period should be limited to five years since this will encompass the majority of claims and the Medicaid look-back period for transfers does not exceed that period. Fourth, work with an independent agent who can provide at least three premium quotes. Some clients end up paying too much due to transactions with captive agents. Fifth, the cost of the insurance may be reduced forty to fifty percent by choosing a home-care only policy — an especially attractive option for clients who either cannot afford complete protection, are willing to rely on Medicaid Planning for Nursing Home protection, or for those over age seventy where the expense tends to be prohibitive.

WHEN IS THE BEST TIME TO PURCHASE COVERAGE?

If you decide that long term care insurance is the right decision to protect your assets and your family's financial future, the best time to buy it is now, because the older you get, the more expensive the policy becomes in the long run. By buying now:

> You avoid the risk of needing care you will have to pay for yourself.

> You avoid the risk of developing a condition that would make you uninsurable later.

> You pay lower premiums now, rather than paying higher premiums later.

The sample table below shows the cost for a 44-year old male of waiting and buying later, assuming that premiums do not change and the applicant remains insurable. The Daily Benefit is increased 5% for each year of waiting, to cover the increased cost of care over time.

Age at Purchase	Daily Benefit	Premium	Premiums Paid to Age 90	Cost of Waiting
44	$200	$1,598	$73,508	$0
46	$221	$1,893	$83,292	$9,784
48	$243	$2,232	$93,730	$20,222
50	$268	$2,643	$105,707	$32,199
52	$295	$3,039	$115,487	$41,979
54	$326	$3,489	$125,607	$52,099

WHAT BENEFITS AND RIDERS ARE MOST IMPORTANT?

The most important benefits are inflation protection, as mentioned above, and a stay-at-home option. Some long-term care insurance policies limit the amount of home care coverage. For example, a policy may pay $200 per day for nursing home care, but only $150 per day for home care; this is an example of a 75% home care benefit. Given that almost everyone needing long-term care prefers to remain in his or her own home for as long as possible, a 100% home care benefit is an essential option.

TAX DEDUCTIBILITY OF LONG-TERM CARE INSURANCE PREMIUMS

Federal Income Tax: Under the Health Insurance Portability and Accountability Act ("HIPAA"), "qualified" long-term care insurance policies receive special tax treatment. To be "qualified," policies must adhere to regulations established by the National Association of Insurance Commissioners:

> The policy must offer the consumer the options of "inflation" and "nonforfeiture" protection, although the consumer can choose not to purchase these features.

> The policies must also offer both activities of daily living ("ADL") and cognitive impairment triggers, but may not offer a medical necessity trigger. "Triggers" are conditions that must be present for a policy to be activated.

> Premiums for "qualified" long-term care policies will be treated as a medical expense and will be deductible from Federal Income Tax to the extent that they, along with other unreimbursed medical expenses (including "Medigap" insurance premiums) exceed 7.5 percent of the insured's adjusted gross income. But the deductibility of premiums is limited by the age of the taxpayer at the end of the year.

State Income Tax: Many states have programs allowing a deduction from state income taxes.

Might The LTC Insurance Company Go Out of Business?

Yes. Several long-term care insurance companies have gone bankrupt. Of course it's important to deal with top-rated companies, but even some top-rated companies have gotten out of the long-term care insurance business in recent years, so buying these policies definitely involves some degree of risk.

chapter **12**

VETERANS AID & ATTENDANCE

T he Department of Veteran Affairs pays for long-term care primarily through its "Aid and Attendance" payments, which is actually a Special Pension with add-on for Aid & Attendance.

ELIGIBILITY REQUIREMENTS

To be an eligible veteran, you must have served 90 days active duty, at least one day during a period of war, and must have not been dishonorably discharged. For a Veteran's surviving spouse to be eligible, the surviving spouse must have been

> ### RELEVANT WARTIME PERIODS:
>
> #### World War II:
> December 7, 1941 - December 31, 1946
>
> #### Korean Conflict:
> June 27, 1950 - January 31, 1955
>
> #### Vietnam Era:
> August 5, 1964 - May 7, 1975; or February 28, 1961 - May 7, 1975 for veterans who served

married for at least one year to the veteran at the time of death or had children with the veteran. Divorce or remarriage excludes qualification.

MEDICAL QUALIFICATION

Once you are determined to be an eligible veteran, the next question is whether you are medically qualified. If you are age 65 and older, there is no requirement to prove disability. However, you or spouse must be in need of regular aid and attendance due to:

> inability to dress or undress yourself, or to keep yourself ordinarily clean and presentable;

> frequent need of adjustment of any special prosthetic or orthopedic appliances which by reason of the particular disability cannot be done without aid (this will not include the adjustment of appliances which normal persons would be unable to adjust without aid, such as supports, belts, lacing at the back etc.);

> inability to feed yourself through loss of coordination of upper extremities or through extreme weakness;

> inability to attend to the wants of nature; or

> incapacity, physical or mental, which requires care or assistance on a regular basis to protect you from hazards or dangers incident to your daily environment.

Not all of the disabling conditions in the list above are required to exist. It is only necessary that the evidence establish that you or your spouse needs "regular" (scheduled and ongoing) aid and attendance from someone else, not that there be a 24-hour need.

If you are not at least 65 years of age or older, then you must be permanently and totally disabled (not due to your own willful misconduct), or a patient in a nursing home, or receiving Social Security Disability benefits.

Determinations of a need for the aid and attendance is based on medical reports and findings by private physicians or from hospital facilities. Authorization of aid and attendance is automatic if evidence establishes the claimant is a patient in a nursing home or that the claimant is blind or nearly blind or having severe visual problems.

NET WORTH QUALIFICATION

There is no set limit on how much net worth a Veteran and his or her dependents can have to qualify financially for the Aid and Attendance benefit. According to the Department of Veteran Affairs, "net worth cannot be excessive." Unfortunately, the VA does not define "excessive," but rather makes the vague and sweeping statement that the decision as to whether a Veteran's net worth is "excessive" depends on the facts of each individual case. The VA says it looks at all of the claimants's assets and determines "if a Veteran's assets are of a sufficient amount that the claimant could live off these assets for a reasonable period of time."

In our firm, we have found that a reasonable amount of money for a Veteran to retain to be ensured of receiving this benefit is approximately $10,000. For Veterans with more money than this, there are numerous asset protection strategies that can we can employ to you and your family legally and ethically protect the excess assets.

MAXIMUM BENEFIT

As of 2013, the maximum possible benefit (i.e., the maximum MAPR) for the Aid and Attendance Benefit is as follows:

• Single Veteran - $20,447 per year (~$1,704/month)

• Married Veteran - $24,239 per year (~$2,020/month)

• Surviving Spouse - $13,138 per year (~$1,095/month)

• Married Vets both w/need - $31,578 per year (~$2,631/ month)

HOW IS THE BENEFIT CALCULATED?

The monthly award is based on VA totaling 12 months of estimated future income and subtracting from that 12 months of estimated future, recurring and predictable medical expenses. Allowable medical expenses are reduced by a deductible to produce an adjusted medical expense which in turn is subtracted from the estimated 12 months of future income.

The net income derived from subtracting adjusted medical expenses from income is called "countable" income or IVAP (Income for Veterans Affairs Purposes). This countable income is then subtracted from the Maximum Allowable Pension Rate -- MAPR -- and that result is divided by 12 to determine the monthly income Pension award. Medical expenses must exceed income by 5% for the maximum benefit. This award is paid in addition to the family income that already exists.

INCOME QUALIFICATION

Many Veterans are mistakenly led to believe that Aid and Attendance is only for Veterans with very low income. The website of the Department of Veterans Affairs says that this program is for "wartime Veterans who have limited or no income." If you speak to a Veterans Service Representative in a regional VA office and ask them about the Veterans Aid and Attendance benefit, they will ask for your household income. When you tell them your household income, they will compare it to a chart and most often tell you that you earn too much income to receive the benefit. While the information they provide may be technically accurate, what they typically don't explain is the "income" for VA purposes (sometimes called IVAP or "adjusted income") is actually your household income minus certain recurring, unreimbursed medical and long-term care expenses. These allowable, annualized medical expenses are such things as health insurance premiums, home health care expenses, the cost of paying a family member or other person to provide care, the cost of adult day care, the cost of an assisted living facility, or the cost of a nursing home.

To be able to receive the Veterans Pension with Aid and Attendance benefit, the veteran household cannot have adjusted income (i.e., household income minus unreimbursed medical expenses) exceeding the Maximum Allowable Pension Rate -- MAPR -- for that veteran's Pension income category. If the adjusted income exceeds MAPR, there is no benefit. If adjusted income is less than the MAPR, the veteran receives a Pension income that is equal to the difference between MAPR and the household income adjusted for unreimbursed medical expenses. The Pension income is calculated based on 12 months of future household income, but paid monthly.

EXAMPLES OF BENEFIT CALCULATIONS

Assume two veterans living in the same assisted living facility, both having the same supplemental health insurance, one with retirement income of $4,880 per month and the other with retirement income of $4,642.70 per month.

Here's the calculation of the Countable Unreimbursed Monthly Medical Expenses for both veterans:

Assisted Living Facility	$4,500.00
Plus Medicare Part B	$99.90
Plus Medicare Supplemental Insurance	$128.00
Equals Total Monthly Unreimbursed Medical Expenses	$4,727.90
Minus 5% of Maximum Benefit ($1,704)	$-85.20
Equals Countable Unreimbursed Monthly Medical Expenses	$4,642.70

Here's the calculation of the IVAP and the total aid & attendance benefit per month for the first veteran:

Total Monthly Income	$ 4,880.00
Less Countable Unreimbursed Medical Expenses	$ -4,642.70
Equals IVAP	$ 237.30

Maximum Aid & Attendance Benefit	$ 1,704.00
Less IVAP	$ -237.30

Equals Total Aid & Attendance Benefit per Month	$ 1,466.70

Here's the calculation of the IVAP and the total aid & attendance benefit per month for the second veteran:

Total Monthly Income	$ 4,642.70
Less Countable Unreimbursed Medical Expenses	$ -4,642.70
Equals IVAP	$ 0.00

Maximum Aid & Attendance Benefit	$ 1,704.00
Less IVAP	$ 0.00
Equals Total Aid & Attendance Benefit per Month	$ 1,704.00

chapter 13

MEDICAID BASICS

A society will be judged on how it treats those in the dawn of life,
those in the twilight of life, and those in the shadow of life.

- Hubert Humphrey

There are many different types of Medicaid, but the Medicaid that will be discussed in this book is the governmental benefits program that pays for Americans who need custodial long-term care, typically provided in nursing homes. Medicaid is funded by federal and state taxes and administered by each state. While the rules for eligibility vary from state to state, the primary benefit of Medicaid is that it will pay for long-term care in a nursing home once an individual has qualified. As mentioned previously, according to AARP about 70 percent of nursing home residents are supported, at least in part, by Medicaid. Most importantly, long-term care paid for by the Medicaid program is legally required to be of the same quality as that of a private pay patient.

> *Healthier lifestyles and advances in modern medicine have been causing Americans to live longer and longer. Unfortunately, this increased life expectancy means that Americans are often out-living their ability to care for themselves.*

The current societal crisis posed by the increasing need for long-term care is a relatively new one. Prior to the advent of nursing homes in the 1950s, those seniors who lived into old age were typically cared for in the homes of their children. Life expectancy was such that most people died before the advent of chronic diseases such as Alzheimer's. Healthier lifestyles and advances in modern medicine have been causing Americans to live longer and longer. Unfortunately, this increased life expectancy means that Americans are often out-living their ability to care for themselves.

Many Americans falsely believe that Medicare will provide chronic/custodial care for themselves and their parents. These people are shocked when they learn the truth — that Medicaid, not Medicare, is the only governmental benefit available to pay for long-term care.

Medicaid, created in 1965 under President Lyndon Johnson, has effectively become the long-term care insurance of the middle class because of the simple fact that very few people can afford to pay the national average of $90,520 per year for a private room or even the $81,030 per year for a semi-private room.[9] As the primary source of nursing home funding in the United States, Medicaid is one of the Federal Government's three "social contracts" with America — the other two being Social Security (which provides retirement income for older Americans), and Medicare (which provides health coverage).

In 2005 Senator Rockefeller, then the ranking member of the Senate Finance Committee's Subcommittee on Health Care, in marking the 40th anniversary of the Medicaid program, stated that

> "President Johnson's noble concept was not just a Democratic ideal; it had been an inspiration shared throughout the early part of the century by legislators and presidents from both parties. And since the signing of the landmark legislation, administrations - both Republican and Democratic - have fought to preserve the Medicaid mission of providing healthcare for the nation's most vulnerable citizens.

> "Sadly, in the past few years, we have seen a misguided, darker view of Medicaid emerge - one that loses sight of its original goal and underlying moral framework. Medicaid has become a scapegoat for the larger ills facing our entire healthcare system. But Medicaid isn't the problem. . . Taking care of our most vulnerable people is a moral obligation.

---

[9] Market Survey of Long-Term Care Costs." November 2012.
http://tinyurl.com/LTC-Survey-2012

"Our representative democracy has a responsibility to do for the future what we have repeatedly done in the past: protect, preserve, and strengthen Medicaid."

APPLYING FOR MEDICAID - WHY YOU NEED HELP

Sixteen years after the creation of Medicaid, the United States Supreme Court called the Medicaid laws "an aggravated assault on the English language, resistant to attempts to understand it." *Schweiker v. Gray Panthers*, 453 U.S. 34, 43 (1981). Thirteen years later, the United States Court of Appeals for the Fourth Circuit called the Medicaid Act one of the "most completely impenetrable texts within human experience" and "dense reading of the most tortuous kind." *Rehabilitation Ass'n of Va. v. Kozlowski*, 42 F.3d 1444, 1450 (4th Cir. 1994). Since then, it has only gotten worse.

> *The United States Supreme Court called the Medicaid laws "an aggravated assault on the English language, resistant to attempts to understand it."*

Congress enacted the Deficit Reduction Act of 2005 on June 23, 2006, retroactive to February 8, 2006, the date of enactment, which rewrote a huge portion of the Medicaid law.

The actual Medicaid application process differs from state to state, but it typically involves filling out a lengthy and detailed application and also submitting appropriate verifications of income, assets, transfers, identity, and citizenship.

Due to tremendous complexity of the Medicaid laws, the Medicaid application process is also extremely complicated, and many persons who file for Medicaid without professional assistance will wind up with the application being rejected for a variety of reasons. Rejection often occurs due to financial issues — either excess resources, excess income, or improperly-timed gifts or transfers. Rejection in many cases is due to missing or incomplete information or verifications. Applications are also sometimes improperly rejected by an eligibility worker (most of whom are underpaid and overworked) who has not had the time to carefully and thoroughly review the application and verifications, or who has improperly applied the legal or financial requirements for eligibility.

The Fourth Circuit has called the Medicaid Act one of the "most completely impenetrable texts within human experience" and "dense reading of the most

Worse yet, an application that is filed at the wrong time can result not only in rejection, but in the imposition of significant penalties against the applicant that could have been avoided by a more timely filing. For these and many other reasons, an experienced elder law attorney should always be hired to represent the applicant through the entire Medicaid process — including planning for eligibility (including, if necessary, Medicaid Asset Protection), preparing and filing the application, working with the local eligibility department during the application and verification process, filing an appeal when necessary, and representing the applicant in connection with any required hearings and appeals.

WHO CAN GET MEDICAID?

Almost anyone can get Medicaid. Medicaid is not a program for poor people. It is a program for anyone who can meet the eligibility criteria. Those criteria will be explained in detail in the next several sections.

OVERVIEW OF MEDICAID ELIGIBILITY CRITERIA

There are four separate but overlapping eligibility criteria for Medicaid, each of which is discussed below in detail:

> Medical Eligibility;

> Resource Eligibility;

> Income Eligibility; and

> Transfer Eligibility.

MEDICAL ELIGIBILITY

To be eligible for Medicaid long-term care assistance in most states, you must generally be "medically needy" – meaning in need of a nursing home level of care, though some states have expanded Medicaid to cover the assisted living level of care. Determination of eligibility for long-term medical care is typically based on a comprehensive needs assessment, which must demonstrate that the proposed Medicaid recipient requires nursing facility services. This individual may have unstable medical, behavioral and/or cognitive conditions, one or more of which may require ongoing nursing assessment, intervention, and/or referrals to other disciplines for evaluations and appropriate treatment. Often adult nursing facility residents have severe cognitive impairments and related problems with memory deficits and problem-solving. These impairments and deficits severely compromise personal safety and, therefore, require a structured, therapeutic environment. Most nursing facility residents are also dependent on others in several Activities of Daily Living (walking; transferring; feeding; dressing; bathing; and toileting).

RESOURCE ELIGIBILITY

In every state, an individual applicant for Medicaid long-term care assistance may have no more than a small amount in "countable resources" in his or her name in order to be "resource eligible" for Medicaid. For example, in Virginia, this Individual Resource Allowance is $2,000. A married couple both applying for Medicaid long-term care assistance may have no more than $3,000 total Resources Allowance in their names in order to be resource eligible for Medicaid.

EXEMPT ASSETS AND COUNTABLE ASSETS

To qualify for Medicaid, applicants must pass some very strict tests on the type and amount of assets they can keep. To understand how Medicaid works, one first needs to learn to differentiate what are known as "exempt assets" from "countable" assets. Exempt assets are those that Medicaid does not take into account. In most states, that includes:

> The applicant's principal residence so long as the equity is below the Home Equity Cap, which is currently $536,000 in most states, but more than $750,000 or more in some states, and is indexed for inflation. However, in some states, such as Virginia, after the nursing home resident has been in the nursing home for a period of time (e.g. six months in Virginia), the resident's home will become a countable resource unless the resident's spouse or other dependent relatives live in the home. When the home is an exempt resource, that means the Medicaid applicant can keep the home and still qualify for Medicaid. But it also means that the home will be part of the Medicaid recipient's estate at death and that the state can therefore exercise Estate Recovery (see page 81) against the home after death, thereby recovering from the sales proceeds of the home some or all of what Medicaid paid during the lifetime of the Medicaid recipient.

> Personal possessions, such as clothing, furniture, and jewelry.

> One motor vehicle, without regard to value.

> Certain property used in a trade or business.

> Certain prepaid burial arrangements.

> Term life insurance policies with no cash value.

> A life estate in real estate (however, the transfer rules on life estates are very complicated and must be carefully observed). Also, in some states, retention of a life estate means that the actuarial value of the life estate immediately prior to death will be considered to part of the Medicaid recipient's estate at death and that the state can therefore exercise Estate Recovery (see page 81) against the home after death, thereby recovering from the sales proceeds of the home some or all of what Medicaid paid during the lifetime of the Medicaid recipient.

> Certain Special Needs Trusts; and

> Certain assets that are considered inaccessible for one reason or another.

All other assets are generally "countable" assets, technically called "resources." Basically all money and property, and any item that can be valued and turned into cash, is a countable asset. This generally includes:

> Cash, savings and checking accounts, credit union share and draft accounts;

> Certificates of deposit;

> Individual Retirement Accounts (IRAs), Keogh plans, 401(k) and 403(b) accounts (though some states exempt retirement accounts if they are in some sort of "payout" status, even though they have a cash value);

> Nursing home accounts;

> Prepaid funeral contracts that can be canceled;

> Certain trusts (depending on the terms of the trust);

> Real estate other than the primary residence;

> Any additional motor vehicles;

> Boats or recreational vehicles;

> Stocks, bonds, or mutual funds; and

> Land contracts or mortgages held on real estate.

ESTATE RECOVERY RULES

Under federal regulations and state laws, the Medicaid agency of every state may make a claim against a deceased Medicaid recipient's estate when the recipient was age 55 or over. The recovery can include any Medicaid payments made on his/her behalf. This claim can be waived if there are surviving dependents. One of the goals of Medicaid Asset Protection is to prevent Estate Recovery.

INCOME ELIGIBILITY FOR MEDICAID

Most people mistakenly think that Medicaid is only for people with very low income. The actual rule for income is that a Medicaid applicant can qualify so long as his gross income is less than the private pay cost of the nursing home care he is receiving. A Medicaid recipient must pay all of his income, less certain deductions, to the nursing home. The deductions include a small monthly personal needs allowance which ranges from around $40 per month to $100 per month depending on the state, a deduction for certain uncovered medical expenses (such as medical insurance premiums) and, in the case of a married applicant, an allowance (called the Community Spouse Resource Allowance) the nursing home spouse may possibly be able to pay to the spouse that continues to live at home. See page 83 for more information about the Community Spouse Resource Allowance.

Some states are "medically needy" states and some states are "income cap" states. In "income cap" states, a Medicaid applicant must have income lower than a specified "cap." However, in those states a special trust, called a Miller Trust (also called a Qualifying Income Trust, a Qualified Income Trust, and Income Cap Trust or and Income Assignment Trust) is needed if the Medicaid applicant's income is above a certain level. The way the Miller Trust works is that after the trust is created, the patient assigns his or her right to receive social security and pension to the trust. In the eyes of the state Medicaid agency, if the Miller Trust is receiving income, the patient is not receiving that income, and thus the excess income "problem" is solved.

THE LOOKBACK PERIOD AND THE TRANSFER RULES

The Lookback Period for Medicaid is 5 years from the date of application. This means that when you file an application for Medicaid, you are asked whether you made any gifts (including charitable donations) or other uncompensated transfers during the 5 years prior to applying for Medicaid. Uncompensated transfers include things such as gambling losses and paying money for someone else's benefit, such as paying for a child's wedding or putting money into a fund for a grandchild's education.

UNCOMPENSATED TRANSFERS AND PENALTY PERIODS

Transfer Penalty. An uncompensated transfer of assets results in a period of ineligibility for Medicaid, typically called a "penalty period." The penalty period begins when (a) the person would be receiving an institutional level of care, (b) an application has been filed, and (c) a person is not in any other period of ineligibility. For most people this means at the time an application is filed and they are receiving care. It is important to understand that the transfer penalty period can be longer than 5 years. Some examples of how the penalty period is calculated are shown in below:

Hypothetical State Penalty Divisor	=	$8,000

Amount Transferred	÷	8000	=	Penalty Period	
$100,000.00	÷	8000	=	12.5	Months
$150,000.00	÷	8000	=	18.8	Months
$250,000.00	÷	8000	=	31.3	Months
$500,000.00	÷	8000	=	62.5	Months

PROTECTIONS FOR THE COMMUNITY SPOUSE

Federal law provides some basic built-in protection for married couples. This law recognizes that it is not fair to completely impoverish both spouses when only one spouse needs to qualify for Medicaid nursing home care.

Community Spouse Resource Allowance (CSRA): All countable assets owned by a married couple as of the "snapshot date" (the first day of the first month that the Medicaid applicant enters the nursing home or becomes "institutionalized," meaning a resident of a hospital and/or nursing home for more than 30 continuous days), regardless of whether titled jointly or in the name of just one spouse, are divided into equal halves. One-half of the countable assets (subject to a current maximum under Federal Law of $115,920 and minimum of $22,184[10]), is then allocated to the Community Spouse. This amount that is allocated to the community spouse is called the "Community Spouse Resource Allowance" or CSRA (sometimes called the Protected Resource Amount or PRA). The remaining assets are allocated to the nursing home spouse, and must be reduced until only the Individual Resource Allowance remains, at which time the nursing home spouse will qualify for Medicaid. The examples below assume a state with a $2,000 Individual Resource Allowance.

> Example 1: John and Mary have $100,000 in combined resources just prior to the date John enters the nursing home. John will be eligible for Medicaid once the couple's combined assets have been reduced to $52,000 ($2,000 Individual Resource Allowance for John plus $50,000 for Mary as her Community Spouse Resource Allowance).

> Example 2: Bill and Nancy have $200,000 in combined resources just prior to the date Nancy enters the nursing home. Nancy will be eligible for Medicaid once the couple's combined assets have been reduced to $102,000 ($2,000 Individual Resource Allowance for Nancy plus $100,000 for Bill as his Community Spouse Resource Allowance).

> Example 3: Sam and Jane have $300,000 in combined resources just prior to the date Sam enters the nursing home. Sam will be eligible for Medicaid once the couple's combined assets have been reduced to $117,920 ($2,000 for Sam plus the maximum of $115,920 for Jane as her Community Spouse Resource Allowance).

---

[10] These amounts are as of January 2013, and are subject to change annually – for updated numbers, see the author's website at
http://www.farrlawfirm.com/keyelderlawnumbers.htm. Some states are more generous and have a higher minimum CSRA, and some always allow the Community Spouse to retain the maximum CSRA, even if it is more than half of the snapshot amount.

Because States are allowed to have laws that are more generous than Federal law, some states automatically allow the Community Spouse to retain the maximum Community Spouse Resource Allowance.

Community Spouse Monthly Income Allowance. Each state allows a possible Community Spouse Monthly Income Allowance, which is a monthly income shift from the Nursing Home Spouse to the Community Spouse. Under Federal law, the Monthly Income Allowance ranges from the MMMNA (Minimum Monthly Maintenance Needs Allowance), currently $1,838.75 per month, to the maximum MMNA, currently $2,898.00 per month[11], and cannot exceed the maximum MMNA unless a court orders support in a greater amount. The Community Spouse Monthly Income Allowance is calculated as follows:

MMMNA (currently $1,891.25) + Excess Shelter Allowance

The Excess Shelter Allowance is the amount by which the Community Spouse's actual shelter expenses[12] exceed the state's "Shelter Standard" (also called the "Housing Allowance").

If the Community Spouse's actual monthly income is lower than the calculated Monthly Income Allowance, the shortfall can be made up from the income of the Nursing Home spouse. Ideally, this extra income will eliminate the need for the Community Spouse to dip into savings each month, which would result in gradual impoverishment.

---

[11] These amounts are as of January 2013, and are subject to change annually – for updated numbers, see the author's website at
http://www.farrlawfirm.com/keyelderlawnumbers.htm. Most states use these numbers, sometimes rounded.

[12] Allowable expenses are: rent; mortgage (including interest and principal); taxes and insurance; condominium or cooperative fees; and the state's Utility Standard deduction, unless utilities are included in the community spouse's rent or condominium or cooperative fees.

EXAMPLE OF MONTHLY INCOME ALLOWANCE

Assume that Mary is the Community Spouse, that her sole source of income is $800 per month in Social Security benefits, and that her actual shelter expenses are $988. First we calculate the Excess Shelter Allowance as follows:

Actual Shelter Expenses	$988.00
Minus Shelter Standard	$-567.38
Equals Excess Shelter Allowance	$420.62

Next, we calculate the MMNA as follows:

Minimum MMNA	$1,891.25
Plus Excess Shelter Allowance	$420.62
Equals MMNA	$2,311.87

Since Mary is entitled to a Monthly Maintenance Needs Allowance of $2,311.87, but only receives $800, she is entitled to receive the shortfall every month from John's Social Security check; this shortfall is called the Community Spouse Monthly Income Allowance.

MMNA	$2,311.87
Less actual income	$-800.00
Equals the Community Spouse Monthly Income Allowance	$1,511.87

The Community Spouse Monthly Income Allowance can be paid to Mary from John's income. The rest of John's income must be paid to the nursing home to partially cover the cost of his care.

chapter **14**

MEDICAID ASSET PROTECTION BASICS

The type of asset protection planning done by most experienced elder law attorneys is known by many names — it is most commonly called Medicaid Asset Protection or just Medicaid Planning, but is also frequently referred to as Benefits-Focused Asset Protection, Long-term Care Planning, Life Care Planning, or Chronic Care Planning.

WHAT IS THE GOAL OF MEDICAID ASSET PROTECTION PLANNING?

The goals that families have for doing Medicaid Asset Protection differ from person to person and family to family. However, it is most important to point out that preserving an inheritance for children is most often not the goal. On the contrary, generally for a married couple the most important goal is to ensure that the spouse remaining at home is able to live the remaining years of his or her life in utmost dignity, without having to suffer a drastic reduction in his or her standard of living. For a single or widowed client, the most important goal is typically to be able to enjoy the highest quality of life possible in the event of an extended nursing home stay. When there is an adult child or grandchild who is disabled, the primary goal is typically to protect assets to be used for the benefit of that disabled family member who is often also receiving Medicaid and Social Security Disability benefits.

Money that is protected through proper planning can be used to provide a nursing home resident with an enhanced level of care and a better quality of life while in a nursing home and receiving Medicaid benefits. For instance, protected assets can be used to hire a private nurse or a private health aide — someone to provide one-on-one care to the resident — to help the resident get dressed, to help the resident get to the bathroom, to help the resident at mealtime, and to act as the resident's eyes, ears and advocate.

Money that is sheltered through proper planning can also be used to purchase things for the nursing home resident or disabled child that are not covered by Medicaid — such as special medical devices, upgraded wheel chairs, transportation services, trips to the beauty salon, etc.

Lastly, a small percentage of clients do have a strong desire to leave a financial legacy for their children or grandchildren, particularly if there is a disabled child or someone who needs special financial help.

An unmarried applicant may have no more than $2,000 in "countable" assets in his or her name in order to be "resource eligible" for Medicaid.

Does this mean that if you need Medicaid assistance, you'll have to spend nearly all of your assets to qualify? No — there are dozens of Medicaid asset protection strategies that can be employed with the help of an experienced elder law attorney. These strategies will be explored in the next two chapters.

chapter 15

LIVING TRUST PLUS™ PLANNING

There are two general types of Medicaid Asset Protection Planning: Pre-Need Planning using the Living Trust Plus™ and Crisis Planning. This chapter will explain the former, and the following chapter will explain the latter.

Pre-need Medicaid Asset Protection Planning is for those persons planning well in advance of the need for nursing home care, while they are still healthy and typically still living independently. These are typically people who do not have long-term care insurance.

Many people erroneously think they can protect their nest eggs through estate planning using a traditional revocable living trust. Although a revocable living trust does a good job of avoiding probate when properly established and funded, an enormous limitation of a revocable living trust is that it does not protect assets whatsoever from creditors or from the expenses of long-term care. For those wishing to protect their assets from general creditors and from the expenses of long-term care, the primary planning option is the Living Trust Plus™ Asset Protection Trust.[13]

Although a revocable living trust does a good job of avoiding probate when properly established and funded, an enormous limitation of a revocable living trust is that it does not protect assets whatsoever from creditors or from the expenses of long-term care.

---

[13] *See* http://www.LivingTrustPlus.com.

Evan Farr created Living Trust Plus™ in 2006, and it's now being used by dozens of exceptional estate planning and elder law attorneys throughout the country, all of whom can be found listed on the website www.LivingTrustPlus.com. For purposes of Medicaid eligibility, the Living Trust Plus™ is the only type of asset protection trust that allows you to retain an interest in the trust while also protecting your assets from being counted against you by state Medicaid agencies.

Whereas the revocable living trust will protect your assets from probate, the Living Trust Plus™ is designed to protect your assets from probate PLUS lawsuits PLUS nursing home expenses. You are a good candidate for the Living Trust Plus™ if you are living independently and have no significant health problems that are likely to require nursing home care within the next five years.

> *Whereas the revocable living trust will protect your assets from probate, the **Living Trust Plus™** is designed to protect your assets from probate **PLUS** lawsuits **PLUS** nursing home expenses.*

Planning with the Living Trust Plus™ offers you the peace of mind of knowing that the assets you place in trust:

> will be protected immediately from lawsuits and other general creditors;

> will be protected for Medicaid purposes (completely after five years, with partial protection possible in less than five years);

> may possibly be used by your beneficiaries to enhance your dignity and quality of life if and when you need nursing home care.

Whatever assets remain in your Living Trust Plus™ will, upon your death, be held for your beneficiaries, free of probate, in a sub-trust designed to protect each beneficiary's inheritance from lawsuits, divorce, and nursing home expenses of the beneficiary.

WHAT IS THE LIVING TRUST PLUS™ ?

The Living Trust Plus™ is an irrevocable asset protection trust that you create as part of your estate planning. The Living Trust Plus™ allows you the ability to receive all ordinary income from the trust financial assets and to use any trust-owned realty or tangible personal property. The only restriction of the Living Trust Plus™ is you can have no direct access to principal (technically called the trust "corpus," which is Latin for "body"). If either you or your spouse have direct access to trust corpus, then all the assets in the trust would be deemed "countable" for Medicaid eligibility purposes and would be completely available to all other creditors. Prohibiting direct access to trust corpus is the key to why the Living Trust Plus™ works. Because you can't withdraw trust corpus, neither may your creditors.

HOW DOES THE LIVING TRUST PLUS™ WORK?

Despite the fact that you can't withdraw trust corpus, you have the ability to retain a very high degree of control over the Living Trust Plus™ assets. In addition to being able to receive all ordinary income from the trust (if desired), you can:

> Live in and use any trust-owned real estate.

> Sell any trust-owned real estate and have the trust purchase replacement real estate if desired.

> Use all trust-owned tangible personal property.

> Sell any trust-owned tangibles and have the trust purchase replacements if desired.

> Drive any trust-owned vehicles.

> Sell any trust-owned vehicles and have the trust purchase replacements if desired.

Additionally, you can:

> Serve as trustee of the Living Trust Plus™ if desired.

> Remove and replace someone else who's serving as trustee of the Living Trust Plus™ .

> Change beneficiaries of the Living Trust Plus™ at any time during your life.

IS THE LIVING TRUST PLUS™ IRREVOCABLE?

Although the Living Trust Plus™ is an "irrevocable" trust, this simply means that you cannot unilaterally revoke the trust. Despite the fact that the trust is irrevocable, it can still be terminated so long as the trustee and all beneficiaries agree to terminate it. Many people, including many misinformed attorneys, erroneously think that the term "irrevocable" means that the trust is set in stone and can never be changed. But, in actuality, the term "irrevocable" means just one thing – that the trust cannot be unilaterally revoked by the trust creator. Although the Living Trust Plus™ is irrevocable and can't be revoked unilaterally by the trust creator, under common law and under the Uniform Trust Code, this type of irrevocable trust can be modified, revoked or partially revoked upon the consent of all interested parties, which is the trust creator, the trustee, and all trust beneficiaries.

WHAT IF YOU NEED SOME OF THE TRUST CORPUS?

Although direct withdrawal of trust corpus from the Living Trust Plus™ is prohibited, there's the potential to indirectly access the trust corpus in two ways. The first way is that the trustee has the ability to make distributions of trust corpus to the trust beneficiaries, who are typically your adult children. If the trustee distributes corpus to a trust beneficiary, that beneficiary can then voluntarily (without any pre-arrangement) return some or all of that corpus or use some or all of that corpus for your benefit. The second way for the settlor to possibly get at the trust corpus is for the trust to be terminated by the agreement of all interested parties as just explained.

The rainiest day possible is the day you wind up in a nursing home, so if you want to truly protect your nest egg and have it actually benefit you when the time comes, you

Also, because The Living Trust Plus™ is designed to permit the trustee to make distributions to beneficiaries, through this mechanism the trustee can stop income payments to a settlor who will be requiring Medicaid in the near future and can avoid estate recovery in those states that use a broad definition of "estate."

There's a graphic illustration of how the Living Trust Plus™ works at www.LivingTrustPlus.com.

WHAT KIND OF ASSETS SHOULD LIVING TRUST PLUS™ OWN?

The main types of assets that can be protected using the Living Trust Plus™ are real estate, including your primary residence, financial investments, ordinary bank accounts, and any life insurance that has cash value. Qualified retirement plans can't be owned by a trust, so to be protected they must first be liquidated and subjected to taxation. This is not necessarily a bad thing if you are over age 59 ½. Regardless of your political persuasion, Congress agreeing to keep taxes low while our country is experiencing the highest debt and deficit in it's history is implausible. Higher taxes are inevitaly in our future until our country gets spending under control. Cash value in your retirement accounts is a countable asset for Medicaid, so the protect those assets by putting them into the Living Trust Plus™ , they must be liquidated and subject to taxation. You can liquidate your retirement accounts now, while taxes are at historic lows, or wait until later and risk that the government will have changed the tax rate you have to pay when you withdraw the money. And don't forget that you WILL have to pay tax on this money. In fact, when you turn 70 ½, the government will force you start taking at least the required minimum distribution (RMD) each year and pay the prevailing tax rates at that time.

The Living Trust Plus™ doesn't affect your retirement income or your primary checking account.

WHY TO USE THE LIVING TRUST PLUS™

Medicaid and Veterans Asset Protection. We live during a time when many baby boomers are taking care of their own parents and children, and consequently putting off planning for their own retirement and long-term care solutions. Furthermore, there are many Americans who can't qualify for long-term care insurance, and these are the ideal candidates for use of the true asset protection capabilities embodied by the Living Trust Plus™ Asset Protection Trust.

The typical clients who use the Living Trust Plus™ are in their mid-60s to mid-80s, already retired, and worried about the potential catastrophic cost of long-term care. They want to protect the nest egg that they've been saving for a rainy day.

Of course, as experienced Elder Law Attorneys, we know that the rainiest day possible is the day you wind up in a nursing home, or even in an assisted living facility, so if you want to truly protect your nest egg and have it actually benefit you when the time comes, you need to do something to protect that money. For the vast majority of Americans, the Living Trust Plus™ is the best way to get this much-needed protection.

> *The typical clients who use the Living Trust Plus™ are in their mid-60s to mid-80s, already retired, and worried about the potential catastrophic cost of long-term care. They want to protect the nest egg that they've been saving for a rainy day.*

The Living Trust Plus™ is a means by which you can transfer the assets you wish to protect to a trust rather than directly to your children. Transfers to trusts provide protection, whereas transfers to adult children are outright gifts. Trusts provide a sense of dignity and security; gifts to children leave you at the mercy of your children and at the mercy of any present or future creditors of your children. Transfer to a Living Trust Plus™ are subject to the Medicaid five-year lookback period previously discussed on page 82. For purposes of Medicaid Asset Protection, the settlor of the trust can retain the right to receive ordinary income or give up that right. For purposes of Veterans Asset Protection, the settlor of the trust must give up the right to receive ordinary income from the trust.

Independence. By transferring assets to a Living Trust Plus™ , income is paid directly to you (if desired) rather than to your children, allowing you to maintain greater financial independence. When your real estate is transferred to a Living Trust Plus™ , you retain the ability to live in the real estate or receive the rental income from the property.

Risk-Avoidance. If a parent transfers assets directly to his children, certain risks must be anticipated: creditors claims against a child; divorce of a child; bad habits of a child; need for financial aid; loss of step-up in basis.

A transfer to a Living Trust Plus™ avoids all of these risks.

Taxation Issues Relating to the Living Trust Plus™ Asset Protection Trust

Income Tax. The Living Trust Plus™ is considered by the IRS to be a "grantor trust." Therefore, the ordinary income of the trust, whether it is paid to the settlor or kept in the trust, is taxed to the settlor at the settlor's tax rate.

Income Tax Reporting. The Rules for reporting income generated by assets owned by the Living Trust Plus™ are contained in the Instructions for Form 1041, under the section entitled "Grantor Type Trusts." The Living Trust Plus™ should obtain a separate tax identification number so that potential creditors, including Medicaid, will clearly see the trust as a separate entity. The trustee does not show any dollar amounts on the form itself dollar; amounts are shown only on an attachment to the form (typically called a Grantor Trust Statement) that the trustee or tax preparer files. The trustee should not use Schedule K-1 as the attachment nor issue a 1099.

Gift Tax. The recipient of a gift never pays gift tax or income tax on the receipt of a gift. The gift tax is a tax that applies only to the giver of a gift, not the recipient. However, because the Living Trust Plus™ is designed so that the settlor retains a limited power of appointment in the trust corpus, transfers to the Living Trust Plus™ are not considered completed gifts for gift tax purposes, and are therefore not subject to gift tax. In any event, with the current gift tax exemption of $5.25 million, most people do not need to be concerned about ever paying any gift tax.

Gift Tax Reporting. Even though the transfer of assets into the Living Trust Plus™ is not considered a taxable gift, pursuant to Treas. Reg § 25.6019-3, a Form 709 U.S. Gift Tax Return should still be filed in the year of the initial transfer into the trust. On the Form 709, the transaction should be shown on the return for the year of the initial transfer and evidence showing all relevant facts, including a copy of the instrument(s) of transfer and a copy of the trust, should be submitted with the return. The penalty for not filing a gift tax return is based on the amount of gift tax due, so if there is no amount due there would be no penalty for failure to file. Nevertheless, a gift tax return should be filed pursuant to Treas. Reg § 25.6019-3. Additionally, the filing of a gift tax return could provide additional evidence to future creditors, including Medicaid, that a completed transfer was in fact made despite the fact that the transfer was not considered by the IRS to be a completed gift for tax purposes.

Gifts from the Trust. Although the transfer to the trust is an incomplete gift for gift tax purposes, if the trustee later distributes trust corpus from the trust to one or more of the beneficiaries, the tax result of such distribution is that a completed gift has now been made from the trust settlor to the beneficiary. Accordingly, a gift tax return should be filed by the settlor for the tax year of such distribution if the amount of such distribution exceeds the annual exclusion amount[14]. This does not mean that gift taxes will have to be paid. Gift taxes do not have to be paid under current law unless you give away more than $5.25 million during your lifetime.

Annual Exclusion Gifts and Lifetime Exemption Gifts. Under the current law[15], the trustee of the Living Trust Plus™ can make an unlimited number of gifts to individuals of up to $14,000 per recipient, per year, and the settlor will not need to file a gift tax return. Additionally, the trustee of the Living Trust Plus™ can give away up to $5.25 million under current law during the lifetime of the Settlor without having to pay any Gift Tax. Many people confuse the **annual gift tax exclusion** with the **lifetime gift tax exemption**, but these are entirely different. Let's try to clear up the confusion:

The Annual Gift Tax Exclusion

The **annual gift tax exclusion** is the amount that can be given away by an individual (or by the trustee of the Living Trust Plus™) in any given year to an unlimited number of people free from any federal gift tax consequences at all. For example, if you have three children, the trustee of the Living Trust Plus™ could give $14,000 to each of your children during the year 2013, and because the total of gifts made to each child during the year is not more than $14,000, these "gifts" to your children will actually not be considered gifts at all for federal gift tax purposes.

The Lifetime Gift Tax Exemption

In addition to the **annual gift tax exclusion**, there is a **lifetime gift tax exemption**, which is the total amount that can be given away, **over and above any annual exclusion gifts**, by an individual (or by the trustee of the Living Trust Plus™) over his or the individual's entire lifetime. The lifetime gift tax exemption

---

[14] The annual gift tax exclusion for the year 2013 is $14,000 per year per gift recipient.

[15] As of 2013.

is tied directly to the federal estate tax exemption so that if you give away any amount of your lifetime gift tax exemption, then this amount will be subtracted from your estate tax exemption when you die. For 2013, the lifetime gift tax exemption is $5.25 million, which is the same as the federal estate tax exemption.

> *Because of how the Living Trust Plus™ is designed, the capital gains exclusion for the sale of the primary residence, as well as the step-up in basis on the settlor's death, are both preserved.*

For example, if the trustee of a Living Trust Plus™ gives away $1 million during the settlor's lifetime, and the Settlor dies in December 2013, then the individual's federal estate tax exemption will only be $4.25 million. Similarly, if the trustee of a Living Trust Plus™ gives away $3 million during the settlor's lifetime, and the Settlor dies in December 2013, then the individual's federal estate tax exemption will only be $2.25 million.

Estate Tax. The corpus of the trust is taxable in the settlor's estate upon death under IRC Section 2036, which says that "[t]he value of the gross estate shall include the value of all property to the extent of any interest therein of which the decedent has at any time made a transfer ... under which he has retained for his life ... the possession or enjoyment of, or the right to the income from, the property."

Step Up in Basis. Because the Living Trust Plus™ is designed so that assets are included in the estate of the Settlor, the trust beneficiaries will receive a step up in tax basis as to trust assets to the fair market value of the assets as of the settlor's death.

Capital Gains Exclusion for Sale of Principal Residence. Since the settlor of the Living Trust Plus™ is considered the owner of the entire trust (including the residence) under IRS Grantor Trust rules, the Settlor is treated as the owner of the residence for purposes of satisfying the ownership requirements of § 121 of the Internal Revenue Code. Accordingly, by transferring a residence to a Living Trust Plus™ , the exclusion from capital gains on the sale of a principal residence is maintained.

chapter 16

REAL LIFE CASE STUDIES

Though some families do spend virtually all of their savings on nursing home care, Medicaid laws do not require it. As outlined in the prior chapters, the Living Trust Plus™ is designed specifically to protect your family's financial security. In this chapter, we will take you through several real-life case studies. First will be a case study of the typical family who is completely unprepared for the worst-case scenario and does no planning whatsoever. Next we'll take a look at a family who prepared well in advance for a long-term care crisis using the Living Trust Plus™. Please note that the following Case Studies represent "short version" scenarios. The kind of planning discussed in these Case Studies must be handled in a very precise manner and must always be done with the assistance of a licensed Living Trust Plus™ attorney.

CASE STUDY 1: PHIL AND JANET – NO PLANNING

Janet and Phil had been married for 48 years when Phil, at age , suffered the first of several strokes. Phil spent 2 years in and out of hospitals and nursing homes for rehab after each stroke. Each time, Medicare, along with Phil's supplemental health insurance, paid for Phil's hospital and rehab stays because he always first spent at least 3 days in the hospital prior to going to the nursing home for short-term rehab. Each time Phil was discharged from short-term rehab, Janet would bring him home and take care of him.

Six months ago, the burden on Janet changed tremendously after Phil had his third and worst stroke, which left him paralyzed on his left side and virtually bedridden, with severe brain damage causing about 80% loss of his short-term memory. Despite the doctor's recommendation to keep Phil in the nursing home for long-term care, Janet, who is age 72, brought Phil home to care for him because Janet thinks they can't afford the nursing home care, which the nursing home told her it is approximately $9,000 per month.

Janet and Phil's assets are their paid-off house, worth about $350,000, and Phil's IRA, which has about $200,000 left in it. As for their income, all they have is their respective Social Security income. Janet knows that Phil could be in the nursing home for many years, and that just two years in the nursing home could wipe out all of their money. If Phil were to be in the nursing for more than two years, she fears she'd have to sell their house to continue paying for Phil's care, and then where would she live? The nursing home admissions director told Janet that after spending all of their money, she could take out a reverse mortgage on their home and use the home equity to continue paying the nursing home, but this option also did not appeal to Janet. Fear and self-preservation kicked in for Janet – she could not help but worry about spending down their limited resources to provide nursing home care for Phil. These emotions joined with love for Phil and a desire to provide him with the best care, which she thought would be care from her, at their home.

WITH PLANNING

What Janet didn't know is that, with the help of a licensed Living Trust Plus™ attorney, she could have planned years ago to protect all of their assets (the house and money) for herself and gotten Phil on Medicaid very quickly to pay for his nursing home care. Or Medicaid could have been used to pay for professional home health care for Phil, sparing Janet the tremendous burden of caring for Phil herself.

So Janet purchased a hospital bed for Phil and set it up in the family room on the main level, in front of the television. With no concern for her own health, Janet has diligently cared for Phil at home for the past 12 months, but this caregiving has taken a huge toll on Janet, both mentally and physically. In addition to doing the things she's always done – shopping, cooking, cleaning, etc. – among her numerous additional duties Janet now has to change

Phil's diapers and his soiled linens several times a day, do at least two extra loads of laundry every day, keep track of and administer Phil's medications, hand feed Phil the special liquid diet that he must be on to avoid choking, and turn him several times a day so he doesn't develop bed sores.

Unfortunately, Janet had never heard of the Living Trust Plus™, and instead went to see the Estate Planning attorney who had drawn up their Wills 15 years ago. All the Estate Planning attorney did was recommend that Phil sign a Power of Attorney and Advance Medical Directive naming Janet, and their son John as an alternate. He also recommended that Janet sign a Power of Attorney and Advance Medical Directive naming their son John, in case something happened to her. The Estate Planning attorney didn't know anything about Elder Law or Medicaid or asset protection or the Living Trust Plus™, and so he didn't offer any relevant advice in that regard, and Janet didn't even know that there were vitally important questions she should be asking about Medicaid and Asset Protection.

Because Phil's needs are so severe, Janet has almost no time for herself. Janet doesn't like to complain, but she has mentioned to her only son, John, that she's always tired, she's not able to get out to see her friends anymore, or to go to church (though she happily still mails in her weekly $100 contribution to the church offering to fulfill their annual pledge). She also confides in John that she cries a lot lately, and that she still worries incessantly about running out of money.

Two weeks ago, Janet fell in the bathtub because she was hurrying, as usual, so as not to leave Phil alone for too long. Janet hit her head on the way down and lost consciousness.

Because neither Phil nor Janet were able to call 911, Janet lay in the bathtub, unconscious, for more than a day before their son, John (after calling and getting no answer for the better part of a morning), drove down on his lunch break to check on them. John found his father in his hospital bed, covered in his own feces and urine because his diapers hadn't been changed in almost two days; Phil was also dehydrated because he hadn't been fed during that time. He found his mother unconscious in the bathtub, and immediately thought she was dead.

Hysterical, John called 911 and the paramedics were there within a few minutes to deal with the situation.

After determining that Janet was alive but unconscious, the paramedics tried to revive her, but with no success. They transported Janet and Phil to the local emergency room, where Janet regained consciousness after 15 hours of observation in the ER. Upon regaining consciousness, Janet's pain was severe, as were her injuries – a severe concussion (which would lead to permanent brain damage and memory loss) a fractured right hip, a bone chip in her left hip, and a broken right arm.

Janet was never the same after this fall. Her memory loss from the brain damage was so bad that it mimicked advanced dementia, and the doctors at the hospital said there was nothing that could be done for her memory. They put a cast on her arm and sent her to the local nursing home for recovery and rehab.

As for Phil, after re-hydrating him at the hospital, he also was sent to the local nursing home for recovery and rehab.

Unfortunately, neither Janet nor Phil had been admitted for 3 days or more to the hospital, and neither Medicare nor their supplemental health insurance would pay for the recovery and rehab. The nursing home told their son, John, that he needed to sign the admission documents for both parents and start paying the $18,000 a month private rate, with the first month due in advance. John dutifully did what the nursing home told him, never stopping to consider if there was an alternative because, like his parents, he had never heard of Elder Law or Medicaid Asset Protection or the Living Trust Plus™.

About 3 months later, when John realized his parents were going to quickly run out of money, he listed their house for sale. Per the recommendation of the real estate agent, John listed the house for sale at $350,000. The tax assessed value of the house was $406,000, but the realtor said in her opinion the actual market value was between $317,000 and $350,000. When the house didn't sell within two months, John started to worry that it wasn't going to sell before his parents ran out of money, so John decided to buy the home himself for $317,000. To get the money to purchase his parent's house, John had to liquidate most of his retirement account and incur the income taxes and a 10% early withdrawal penalty, but he figured this was better than having to pay $18,000 per month for the care of his parents once their money ran out.

John put the proceeds from the sale of his parents' home in their bank account and continued to use this money to pay the nursing home bills.

About eighteen months later, Phil and Janet were still in the nursing home, and all of their money was gone. The nursing home told John he needed to apply for Medicaid for his parents. Without giving a single thought to hiring an attorney or even seeking legal advice, John applied for Medicaid as the nursing home told him to.

The first time John applied, even though he spent more than 25 hours over a weekend completing the Medicaid applications, both parents were denied Medicaid because John had failed to fill out the applications properly.

WITH PLANNING

With the help of an experienced Elder Law attorney, this result could have been avoided. Filing for Medicaid is one of the most complex and nightmarish endeavors in existence, and should never be undertaken without first consulting with an experienced Elder Law Attorney. In my firm, we fill out Medicaid applications for our clients every day to avoid the perils and pitfalls that people encounter when trying to file for Medicaid on their own.

The second time John applied, both parents were denied Medicaid again because John failed to provide the Medicaid agency with all of the documentation and verifications that they requested in connection with the sale of his parents' home and in connection with their charitable gifts, as the agency requested this at the last minute and John did not have time to hunt down and obtain the required documents.

WITH PLANNING

With the help of an experienced Elder Law attorney, this result could have been avoided. Our firm, for example, ensures that all required documentation is provided to us before we file the Medicaid application, so our clients don't

---

In the meantime, the nursing home bills were already piling up at the rate of $18,000 per month since Phil and Janet's money had run out, and the nursing home billing department was calling John at home and at work at least once a week, threatening to sue John for the outstanding nursing home bills if he did not make payment immediately. Finally they turned the outstanding bills ($54,000 for 3 months of nursing home care) over to a collection agency, which harassed John and threatened to destroy his credit.

At the same time John was receiving dunning notices from the collection agency, he was being told by the nursing home administrator that his parents were going to be discharged from the nursing home for failure to pay, and that it was John's responsibility to take them home and take care of them, as he had signed the nursing home contracts as the "Responsible Party" for both of his parents.

The third time John applied, he provided all of the requested documentation, and the Medicaid Agency finally approved Medicaid for both parents, but assessed a penalty period of 20 months. This penalty period was incurred because John's parents had made $26,000 in charitable gifts in the last 5 years, and because John had sold their house for $89,000 less than the tax assessed value (which Medicaid considers to be equivalent to a gift to the buyer of the home – in this case John – in the amount of $89,000). The total gifts of $115,000 were divided by the penalty divisor in their state, which was 5750, resulting in a 20-month penalty period, meaning a 10- month period of Medicaid ineligibility for each of his parents. This meant that although John's parents had no money left, Medicaid would not pay for their nursing home care for 10 months.

Who did have to pay for the nursing home during that time? According to the nursing home, John did, because he signed the nursing contract as the "Responsible Party" and because he was the recipient of the $89,000 gift in connection with the sale of the home. So John had to pay 10 months of nursing home costs for the care of his parents, at $18,000 per month. This was a total of $180,000 that John had to pay as a penalty for trying to help his parents.

WITH PLANNING

With the help of an experienced Elder Law attorney, all of these bad results could have been avoided. The following Case Studies will demonstrate the benefits of proper planning.

CASE STUDY 2: GLENDA – PLANNING IN ADVANCE WITH THE LIVING TRUST PLUS™

Three years ago, Brenda's husband died after suffering a massive stroke. Although Brenda's husband had died quickly and had not needed to spend time in the nursing home after his stroke, Brenda has many friends whose spouses spent significant time in nursing homes prior to their death, and Brenda knows, through these friends, of the financial devastation that is caused by prolonged nursing home stays. Although devastated over the loss of her husband, Brenda is also glad that he did not have to spend any time in a nursing home, because she knows that a prolonged nursing home stay could have bankrupted her.

Although Brenda is 85-years old, she is still quite healthy, and able to live independently. The only thing that Brenda can't do is drive, because she has macular degeneration that is causing her eyesight to fail. Luckily, Brenda's oldest daughter, Jane, lives nearby and is retired, so Jane is able to take Brenda where she needs to go.

After the death of her father, one of the first places Jane takes her mom is to the attorney who did their estate planning documents years before her father had died, to see what needs to be done, if anything, about her father's estate. Jane and Brenda are happy to learn that only minimal work needs to be done because all of the assets of her parents were titled jointly, and would pass to Brenda automatically with proper notification of her husband's death.

Since they are at the lawyer's office, Brenda asks if there is anything that could be done to protect her assets against the possibility that she might some day need nursing home care. (Brenda's primary reason for wanting protect her assets is to preserve her own future dignity and quality of life; she is not concerned about leaving a large inheritance to her children because all of her children are financially well-off in their own rights.) Although the lawyer is not Living Trust Plus™ Attorney, he has heard of the Living Trust Plus™ and suggests that Brenda and Jane look into it as a method of accomplishing the asset protection they are interested in.

That evening, Jane helps Brenda look up the name of a Living Trust Plus™ Attorney by going to www.LivingTrustPlus.com, and they find that the Living Trust Plus™ Attorney in their area is offering an informational seminar the following weekend, so they sign up for seminar. At the seminar, Jane and Brenda learn all about the Living Trust Plus™ as a method of Medicaid Asset Protection (see page 91), and decide they wanted to pursue it further, so they make an appointment for a free consultation with the attorney.

Once the attorney confirms that Brenda is an appropriate candidate for the Living Trust Plus™, Brenda goes ahead and has the attorney prepare one for her, and Brenda also had the attorney transfer her house, which worth about $340,000 and is her major asset, into the Living Trust Plus™. Brenda decides that she will keep her $97,000 IRA, which is her only other significant asset, out of the trust.

For the next four years, Brenda remains relatively healthy, and is able to live day to day on her $1,200 per month retirement income plus minimum distributions from her IRA. Jane spends just 4 or 5 hours a week helping Brenda pay her bills and balance her checkbook (her dad had always done that before his death) and driving Brenda to her medical appointments. On February 10, six days short of her 90th birthday, Brenda trips and falls and breaks her hip. After 3 days in the hospital and 4 weeks of rehab in a local nursing home, it becomes clear that Brenda needs to stay at the nursing home for long-term care.

Jane knows that her mom only has about $80,000 left in her IRA, and at $9,200 per month for the nursing home, Jane knows the IRA money will only last about another 10 months. Jane returns to the attorney who drew up Brenda's Living Trust Plus™ to see what can be done.

The attorney explains that Brenda should go ahead and use the remaining IRA money to pay for the first 10 months of nursing home care. Although the IRA distributions are subject to income tax, the tax incurred will be offset by Brenda's nursing home bills which qualify for the medical expense deduction, so little or no taxes will actually have to be paid.

During this 10-month period, Brenda's lawyer explains that Jane, as Trustee of her mother's Living Trust Plus™, should sell her mom's former residence. The $340,000 or so in proceeds from the sale of the former residence will go into Brenda's Living Trust Plus™ and Jane, as Trustee, can decide how to invest these proceeds – whether in CDs, mutual funds, stocks, bonds, etc.

At the end of this 10-month period, Brenda will not have any money left to pay for the nursing home. However, the lawyer explains that Jane could then make a "back door" distribution as Trustee of her mother's Living Trust Plus™ of about $16,000 in trust assets as a gift to herself and then Brenda could, if she wishes, voluntarily use that gifted money to help her mother pay for the next two months of nursing home care. Assuming Jane were to do this, then at the end of said two month period, the Medicaid 5-year lookback period will have elapsed and the remaining $324,000 in her mother's Living Trust Plus™ will be protected from being counted when applying for Medicaid to pay the remaining nursing home bills for the rest of Brenda's life.

At the end of this 10-month period, Brenda will not have any money left to pay for the nursing home. However, Jane can make "back door" distributions as Trustee of her mother's Living Trust Plus™ to pay for her mother's nursing home care until the expiration of the 5-year

chapter 17

MEDICAID CRISIS PLANNING

Medicaid Crisis Planning is for families with a loved one who has already entered, or is about to enter, a nursing home, and it is expected that the nursing home resident will not be able to return home. If this describes your family, you need to know that there are dozens of asset protection strategies that can be used, under the direct and ongoing supervision of a qualified and experienced elder law attorney, to protect your family's assets and obtain Medicaid benefits. This type of Planning provides comprehensive Medicaid Asset Protection, including completion and filing of the Medicaid application and all documents and actions required to obtain Medicaid. When appropriate, Veterans Benefits Planning and the filing of a Veterans Aid and Attendance Pension application can also be done. This type of planning provides a client with: a written Asset Protection Plan (APP); all appropriate asset protection documents; all research, conferences, advice, expertise, and other services necessary to achieve the desired goals; supervised execution of all documents required under the APP; and unlimited consultations between you and our attorneys and staff as necessary to design and implement the APP

> With Medicaid Crisis Planning, if you're a married couple and one spouse is healthy and living at home, as a general rule 100% of your assets can be protected for the healthy spouse, regardless of how the assets are titled. If you're not married, the general rule is that 40% to 70% of your assets can be protected.

consistent with your needs, goals, and desires, and to carry out the APP to completion prior to our filing for Medicaid and/or Veterans Pension benefits.

HOW MUCH CAN BE PROTECTED?

If you're a married couple and one spouse is healthy and living at home, as a general rule 100% of your assets can be protected for the continued use and benefit of the healthy spouse, regardless of how the assets are titled. If you're not married, as a general rule 40% to 70% of your assets can be protected. In addition to the Asset Protection, your Elder Law Attorney should assist you when needed with selection of care facilities, review all paperwork prior to signing, and represent you in connection with any threatened discharge from a care facility.

The asset protection strategies used under this Level of Planning break down into two broad categories – Asset Purchase Strategies (also called "smart spenddown") and Asset Transfer Strategies.

A list of sample Asset Purchase Strategies and Asset Transfer Strategies is provided below.[16]

SAMPLE ASSET PURCHASE STRATEGIES AVAILABLE IN MOST STATES

> Prepayment of legal or other services;

> Payment for home improvements if home is exempt;

> Purchase of household goods and personal effects;

> Purchase of a more expensive home if the home is exempt;

> Purchase life estate and reside for one year;

> Purchase of pre-paid funeral arrangements;

> Purchase of a new car;

> Prepayment of taxes;

---

[16]Most of these strategies are based on federal law, but none of these strategies should be attempted without the direct and ongoing supervision of an experienced and qualified elder law attorney who has both (1) a comprehensive understanding of each strategy's specific rules and requirements in your state and (2) a thorough understanding of each strategy's Medicaid, estate planning and tax consequences (including income tax and capital gains tax).

> Payment of outstanding debts;

> Purchase of a special Medicaid-compliant annuity.

SAMPLE ASSET TRANSFER STRATEGIES AVAILABLE IN MOST STATES

> Transfer assets to blind or disabled child;

> Transfer assets to a trust for the sole benefit of a blind or disabled child;

> Transfer residence to caregiver child;

> Transfer residence to sibling on title for more than a year;

> Transfer residence subject to life estate;

> Transfer residence subject to occupancy agreement;

> Caregiver agreement between parent and child;

> Transfer and Cure.

For more information on Medicaid Crisis Planning, please see the book **"Nursing Home Survival Guide,"** by Evan H. Farr,

chapter 18

FINDING THE RIGHT LAWYER

The way to find a Living Trust Plus™ lawyer is simply by going to the Living Trust Plus™ Web site at www.LivingTrustPlus.com and clicking on "Find an Attorney." There you will find a listing of the dozens of experienced and expert attorneys around the country who have been licensed by Evan Farr and trained in the proper use and creation of the Living Trust Plus™ Asset Protection Trust.

Unfortunately, there are not yet have attorneys in every state who are authorized to offer the Living Trust Plus™. However, we are continuously in the process of growing the Living Trust Plus™ network by adding additional attorneys to work with us in offering the Living Trust Plus™ Asset Protection System, and we will be happy to work with you in trying to find an attorney in your local area.

If you are interested in the Living Trust Plus™ but do not have a local attorney, there is a contact form on the website at www.LivingTrustPlus.com that you can use to contact us, or you can call our toll-free hotline at 1-800-399-FARR and let us know if you have a local Estate Planning or Elder Law attorney you have worked with in the past, or a specific local attorney you have identified as someone you would possibly like to work with in the future. If you are able to provide us with the name of a local attorney you would like to work with, then we will be happy to contact that attorney to explore whether we can work with that attorney to provide you with the Living Trust Plus™ Asset Protection Trust. Or you can direct that attorney to the LivingTrustPlus.com website and have the attorney check out the "For Attorneys" section of the web site. You can also refer them to the book entitled the "Attorney's Guide to the Living Trust Plus™ Asset Protection Trust" which provided an in-depth education to the attorney about the legalities of how and why the Living Trust Plus™ Asset Protection Trust works.

If you have more than one local attorney who you'd be comfortable working with, please provide us with the name and contact information for each such attorney. If you have not identified any local attorneys that you'd like to work with, don't worry. We can still try to recruit an attorney to work with us in offering the Living Trust Plus™ in your local area. In that regard, it would be very helpful to us if you could provide us with a list of each City or Town in your state that is geographically close to you.

Once we have obtained the above information from you, we can then start by reaching out to attorneys whose offices are convenient for you to travel to, and we will let you know if and when we have found an attorney who you can work with. Alternatively, our firm would be pleased to assist you directly.

ABOUT THE AUTHOR

Evan Farr, Certified Elder Law Attorney, is the creator of the Living Trust Plus™ Asset Protection System and is widely recognized as one of the foremost experts in the Country in the field of Medicaid Asset Protection and Medicaid Asset Protection Trusts. Evan has been quoted or cited as an expert by numerous sources, including the Washington Post, Newsweek Magazine, Trusts & Estates Magazine, The American Institute of Certified Public Accountants, and the American Bar Association, and is a frequent guest on various local and national radio shows. Evan received a Psychology degree from the University of Pennsylvania in 1984 and his law degree from the College of William & Mary in 1987.

Evan is the recipient of the highest ratings awarded by all the attorney-rating services: Best Lawyers in America, Super Lawyers, Avvo, and Martindale-Hubbell. In 2011, Evan was named by Washingtonian Magazine as one of the top attorneys in the DC Metropolitan area, by Northern Virginia Magazine as one of the top attorneys in the Northern Virginia area, and by Newsweek Magazine as one of the top attorneys in the country.

Evan is a nationally renowned Best-Selling author and frequent educator of attorneys across the U.S. As an expert to the experts, Evan has educated tens of thousands of attorneys across the country through speaking and writing for organizations such as his own Elder Law Institute for Training and Education (ELITE), the National Academy of Elder Law Attorneys, the American Law Institute-American Bar Association, the National Constitution Center, the National Business Institute, the Virginia Academy of Elder Law Attorneys, the Virginia Bar Association, Virginia Continuing Legal Education, and the District of Columbia Bar Association. His numerous publications include a Best-Selling book, *Protect and Defend*, as well as hundreds of articles that have appeared in the popular press, and dozens of scholarly publications for the legal profession, including two legal treatises published by the American Law Institute in affiliation with the American Bar Association: *Planning and Defending Asset Protection Trusts* and *Trusts for Senior Citizens*.

Virginia has no procedure for approving certifying organizations.

Made in the USA
Charleston, SC
14 April 2015